D0062549

A

NEGLECTED

GRACE

Family Worship
in the Christian Home

Jason Helopoulos

Scripture quotations are from *The Holy Bible, English Standard Version*, copyright © 2001 by Crossway Bibles, a division of Good News Publishers. Used by permission. All rights reserved. ESV Text Edition: 2007.

Jason Helopoulos is assistant pastor at University Reformed Church in East Lansing, Michigan, and a guest blogger at The Gospel Coalition. He is ordained in the Presbyterian Church in America. He and his wife, Leah, are parents of two young children, Gracen and Ethan.

Copyright © Jason Helopoulos 2013

paperback ISBN 978-1-78191-203-4
epub ISBN 978-1-78191-237-9
mobi ISBN 978-1-78191-238-6

10 9 8 7 6 5 4 3 2 1

Published in 2013
by
Christian Focus Publications, Ltd
Geanies House, Fearn,
Ross-shire, IV20 1TW, Scotland
www.christianfocus.com

Cover design
by
Daniel van Straaten

Printed by
Bell and Bain, Glasgow

Just what I needed! An encouraging refresher on family worship that reminded me of the "Why?" and gave me lots of new ideas about "How?" Also a powerful motivation and perfect guide for parents just starting this much-blessed practice, with lots of practical and realistic tips.

David P. Murray
Professor of Old Testament and Practical Theology, Puritan Reformed Theological Seminary
Grand Rapids, Michigan

Family worship is a true blessing! This excellent book will open your eyes to see why it is a missing DNA of Christian lifestyle. It gives you a complete picture of why, what, who, where, when and how to reinstall this missing DNA. More than that, this book helps you to remove all the obstacles away from having a good family worship and gives you lively personal stories. I have started a family worship with my wife and two sons after reading this inspiring book.

Silas Ng
Missionary Bishop of Canada
Anglican Mission in the Americas, Richmond, British Columbia, Canada

The revival of family worship is one of the most encouraging developments in modern Christianity. However, the practice is still rare. Most Christian homes are still void of anything resembling the family altar that once represented the norm among Christ's followers. Few in our day have ever seen or experienced family worship. Rich in both theological reflection and practical application, *A Neglected Grace*, is a welcome and much-needed tool for those keen on reviving these practices in their own homes, or being an encouragement to others. Even more encouraging than the content of this book is the prospect that its readers will embrace and employ these timeless practices and honor God in their homes.

Voddie Baucham, Jr.
Pastor of Preaching, Grace Family Baptist Church, Author of *Family Driven Faith*, and
Family Shepherds, Spring, Texas

CONTENTS

Foreword by Kevin DeYoung....................................11

Introduction...13

1: Worshipers: Who We Are/
   Worship: What We Do 19

2: Give Me A Reason!
   It's Our Joyful Responsibility!....................................29

3: How About Some Other Practical Reasons?.............41

4: Now What? What Do I Do? 51

5: Our Manner of Worship 67

6: What Family Worship is Not 73

7: Helps for the Journey..81

8: But, What if… 89

9: Just Do It...99

Appendices: Family Worship Templates and Helps

   Appendix A: Sample Family Worship Structures..........111

   Appendix B: Simple Beginnings with Scripture
               and Prayer 115

   Appendix C: Resources..121

   Appendix D: Catechisms and Creeds............................125

To Leah, Gracen and Ethan

Thank you for making it a joy to come home and sorrowful to leave. I am blessed beyond measure.

Foreword

Right near the top of the list of things I really want to do, but struggle to do well, would be family worship. I know it's important, but seem to fail as much as I succeed. Family worship will burst on the scene for five days, only to disappear for four. The kids will enthusiastically participate one night and barely sit still the next. Family worship is something my wife and I have done with our kids for years and something we've struggled with just as long. It's hard to be consistent, hard to be creative, hard to make the time, hard to make the kids pay attention, hard to push through seeming tedium to the point of supernatural triumph.

Which is why I love this book.

I love the title: *A Neglected Grace*. Instead of hammering us with the heavy hand of ought, Jason holds out family worship as an example of divine kindness. Yes, we need motivation for the discipline of family worship, but the best, longest-lasting motivation comes not by feeling terrible for what we could be doing better, but by believing what good God has in store for us. The message of the book isn't "Pray with your family or else!" but "Think of how sweet this will be".

I love the practicality of this book. Jason has reached back into the history of the church without sacrificing relevance for our own day. His reflections are timeless, and his counsel is timely. He doesn't just tell us what to do. He shows us how to do it. Jason gives us questions to ask, elements to try, books to read, hymnals to consult, and real life stories from which to learn. I expect everyone who reads this book will walk away with two great conclusions: "I want to grow in family worship" and "I have some great next steps to take in that direction".

Finally, and on a subject like this, maybe most importantly: I love the good friend of mine who wrote this book. In a day where we have hundreds of "friends" on Facebook and introduce every acquaintance as "My good friend so and so", I count it a privilege to have Jason as a real, flesh and blood, stick by you no matter what, friend. He's a good pastor, a good husband and a good father. He'd be the first to tell you he's not perfect—not with family worship or anything else. But that doesn't mean he's not a example to follow. This is one pastor who practices what he preaches. I know firsthand that he writes as one who takes seriously all the challenges and all the opportunities fleshed out in this excellent book. The "neglected grace" of family worship is not neglected in his home.

And that's a man I can respect, with a book I need.

Kevin DeYoung
March 2013

Introduction

It's gone! Or, at the very least, it is rarely seen or heard. If it were an animal, it would be on the endangered species list. We have not only stopped *doing* it, but we have stopped *talking* about it. We hear few sermons or pastoral exhortations that attend to it. We find few fathers and mothers encouraging one another to pursue it. Christian publications seem to have forgotten about it altogether. And yet, in the history of the church, it has been one of the Christian family's strongest characteristics: That is why this book includes a number of quotes from Christians of previous centuries.

What is it that was part of the DNA of the Christian family in previous centuries, but seems to have all but vanished in this past century? Family worship. This glorious expression of our Christian faith used to mark Christian homes, but over the past one hundred years, the evangelical church seems to have forgotten about it. It is time for us to explore and promote family worship in the church again. We need to hear about the need for family worship in our homes. Pastors need to stress the importance of it. And laypeople need to be talking about it. But even more importantly, we need to begin to practice it, so that this silent void which has crept into our Christian homes will disappear. My hope is that our Christian homes will once again be filled with fathers, mothers, husbands, wives, children, sisters, and brothers that are worshiping to the glory of God.

When I think of Christian homes, I always think of the city of Kidderminster, England, in the seventeenth century. Kidderminster was a small city which contained around 800 homes and 2,000 people. It was to this city that Richard Baxter was called as a minister. Baxter's ministry in this city had a great effect.[1] Baxter reports that, when he arrived in Kidderminster, the town was made up of an "ignorant, rude, and reveling people"[2] However, the Lord blessed the preaching of His Word in this town, and many came to saving faith.

One of the great transformations that occurred in the city after this awakening was the blossoming of family worship. Baxter says of this change that, "On the Lord's days…you might hear a hundred families singing psalms and repeating sermons as you passed through the streets…when I came thither first there was about one family in a street that worshiped God and called on his name, and when I came away there were some streets where there was not past one family in the side of a street

---

1   Richard Baxter was one of the great Puritan preachers of the seventeenth century. He was one of the best writers and thinkers in Puritan circles on practical Christian living. However, not everything of Baxter's ministry or pen is to be commended.

2   Quoted in J.I. Packer's "Introduction" to *The Reformed Pastor* by Richard Baxter (Carlisle, PA: Banner of Truth Trust. Reprinted in 1999.), p. 11.

that did not so...."[3] Homes that were once places of darkness and unbelief were transformed into places of light and worship. If one walked the streets of Kidderminster on a Lord's Day evening, after the families had attended the morning worship services at church, the sound of children and parents worshiping together would flow from the open windows into the night sky. Worshiping in their homes was one of the natural responses of these individuals and their families upon their conversion. They desired to gather with their families and worship the Lord who saved them. Could anything be more appropriate and right?

This is a small and simple book. And I have a small and simple prayer to accompany it. It is my hope that the Lord will use this book to encourage you and your family to introduce family worship in your home or to persevere in it. There is no better time than now for this time-tested and beneficial aspect of the Christian life to be revived.

However, my hopes for a revival of family worship are not meant to place burdensome expectations on Christian homes. I recently received a note from a mother who said, "You know, there are times when many Christian parents feel a sense of condemnation for not having regular (worship) with their kids. I know I have felt that way at times, which was why I would try to do something along those lines and yet I did not succeed." We all know well that sense of struggle and, at times, failure, in leading our homes in worship. At the outset, I want to make it clear that this book is not intended to heap guilt upon the shoulders of husbands, mothers, or parents who have struggled to lead their homes in family worship. My great challenge in writing this book was to do so in a way that would show the benefits of family worship—how important

---

3   Ibid, p. 12.

and beneficial it is for the Christian family—and yet would do so in a way that would not lead struggling husbands, fathers, and mothers to be weighed down by guilt. If this book increases guilt in the reader, then my prayer is that it quickly goes out of print. Instead, I hope that this book will be an encouragement to the reader to have a true resolve to engage in family worship, but only by, in, through, and because of the grace of God. As we approach the subject of family worship it is helpful to be reminded that it is nothing more than our response in the home to God's magnificent and infinite grace. And it is by that grace that we gather together with our family members to delight in His excellent goodness and eternal glory. Family worship is not something we have to do. Our right standing before God is not impacted by whether we lead our families in worship or not. Christ has already accomplished all for our salvation. Rather, family worship, like other spiritual disciplines, becomes something we *want* to do. As the individual Christian, changed by God's grace, naturally begins to read the Bible, sing, and pray, so the Christian family impacted by the grace of God will want to gather together to read the Bible, sing, and pray. As all the Christian life is lived in grace, so we enjoy and pursue family worship by that same grace.

I am not an expert in family worship. My wife and kids can testify to that. My family and I continue to learn how to do family worship better, more faithfully, more consistently, and with more joy. I confess that it is not always easy, and at times it even seems laborious. But I have seen up-close the fruit that accrues in a family when they worship regularly together in their home. Family worship has benefits that are eternal; and that is worthy of our pursuit. Consider this book an encouragement to that end.

The following chapters present a sound theological and biblical basis for family worship, supplemented with very practical everyday advice for implementing this practice in our homes. Much of this material has been developed as a result of my own struggles and successes at home as well as those of the families I have had the privilege to minister with and to. Chapter one takes a look at the purpose for which we were created and recreated in Christ Jesus. We are worshipers, and this is the dominant factor for all of our life. Chapter two wrestles with our particular responsibility to engage in family worship. Chapter three rounds out the opening chapters with some additional practical reasons to begin this beneficial discipline.

Some of you may already be convinced of the call to worship with your family and the benefits which flow from it. However, you may be struggling to implement this important activity on a regular basis. If that is the case, then you may want to skip the first few chapters and begin in chapter four, where this book begins to detail the practicalities of family worship, its means, manner (Ch. 5), and what family worship is not (Ch. 6). Chapters seven through nine provide some added helps for implementing family worship and attempts to answer common objections to our struggles with beginning it. In chapter ten, the reader will find helpful testimonials from families honestly engaging and struggling to practice family worship in the home.

Dear Christian, as you read this book, be reminded that Christ is your joy and salvation. He delights in you, and family worship is yet another daily opportunity for us to delight in Him with those we most love in this life. May we be the generation that reinvigorates this storied and beneficial characteristic of the Christian life for the good of ourselves, our families, and the generations to come.

CHAPTER 1

Worshipers: Who We Are
Worship: What We Do

Everyone lives for something. That is reality. We may not be aware of what we are living for, but we are living for something. And what we live for naturally shapes our daily lives. Some people live to accrue a large savings account. Therefore, they labor every day to store up money. Some people's *raison d'être* is their family. Everything begins to circulate around raising their children, so soccer games, ballet lessons, and Boy Scout meetings dictate each week. Some people live for relaxation and self-pleasure. They tend to live life by the motto, "Just get through today." They can't wait to get home and slump down in front of the television. Recently, I was in a video game store buying a present for someone and overheard an employee of the store comment that he couldn't wait to get home to play a particular video game. He then made the bold declaration, "I believe I was put on earth to play this game." Everyone lives for something. And this something shapes our daily activities. However, not all reasons for living are equal.

I, for one, am thankful that we weren't created just to play video games. Don't get me wrong—I enjoy a good video game, but there has to be something more to life than squashing mushrooms and freeing Princess Toadstool. If we weren't created for video games, then what were we created for? There is nothing more crucial for our understanding of life than the fact that we were created by God to worship Him. This is at the very heart of what it means to be human. People may live life as if their reason for existing were something else, but all of us were created to worship God. Adam was created from the dust of the ground to be a worshiper. Eve was created from his side to be a worshiper. This is who man is and this is what man was created for. Yet, this is not always how we live our lives or what we understand to be our ultimate purpose. Why is that? Because sin has had its effects. In Adam's choice to eat of the fruit of the tree of knowledge of good and evil, man chose to ignore and rebel against God's calling (Genesis 3). Instead of worshiping God by resting in dependence upon Him and obeying His command, man chose to seek independence from God and thwart His rule.

Adam went from being a worshiper who enjoyed the fellowship of God to a rebel raising his fist in defiance of God. In fact, our first parents, Adam and Eve, did not just choose to forsake worshiping God; they chose to worship something altogether different: self. The great sin of the Garden of Eden is fundamentally an exchange in the object of worship. And all mankind fell with them in that first sin. All of human history could be described as a story about worship. Will man worship God as he was created to do? Will he be a worshiper in spirit and truth (John 4)? Or will man worship the creation and self rather than the Creator (Rom. 1)? This is the great drama of human history.

What a fateful decision Adam and Eve made on that day. And yet, our God was not content to allow all of His creation to be silent in praise. Therefore, God chose to redeem a people for Himself that we might worship Him forever. God Himself, in the person of the Son, became flesh, lived, suffered, and died that we might be set free from the guilt, penalty, and power of sin. Christians are those whom He has saved "to the praise of His glory" (Eph. 1:12). This is the reason we were created and the reason we were recreated! This is our reason for being. This is our highest calling and our eternal purpose: to worship Him. But for the Christian, it is even more than our highest calling and eternal purpose: it is our heart's desire. We have a redeeming God, who has poured out His love upon us. For God has shown His "love for us in that while we were still sinners, Christ died for us" (Rom. 5:8). Worship is not something we *have* to do, it is something we *want* to do. If we understand what He has done for us, we cannot help but love and worship Him. It is a thankful and grace-changed heart that seeks God in worship.

WORSHIP IN ALL OF LIFE

As we think about worshiping God, it is true that we are to "worship Him in all of life." This is made clear in passages such as Romans 12:1, in which we are told "to present [our] bodies as a living sacrifice," and 1 Corinthians 10:31, where the Apostle Paul tells us, "whether you eat or drink, or whatever you do, do all to the glory of God." As Christians, our lives are to be a continual act of worship. However, in recognizing this, we must be careful that we do not negate or diminish the importance of specific times of worship. In the history of the church and the history of God's people in Scripture, there have always been three clearly defined spheres of worship: secret

21

worship, corporate worship, and family worship.[1] We will briefly review these types of worship below before focusing more fully on family worship.

First Sphere—Secret Worship

Secret worship is the first sphere of worship in the Christian's life. Secret worship is that individual, private worship that we do in our closets and behind closed doors. In recent years, the importance of secret worship has been highlighted in the Western evangelical church with an emphasis upon "daily quiet times." However, the idea of secret worship is not something new. We see this type of worship emphasized in the history of God's people throughout the Scriptures. We witness it in God's commission of Joshua after the death of Moses and His exhortation to meditate upon the Law day and night (Josh. 1:8). It is evidenced in Daniel's willingness to face a possible death sentence to maintain a daily time of worship with the Lord (Dan. 6). We observe it frequently in the Psalms as they speak of worshiping God as part of our daily living, even during the watches of the night upon our bed (Ps. 63:6; 77:6; 119:148).

In the New Testament, we encounter a man named Cornelius. He is described as "a God-fearing man", who is marked by a spirit of prayer (Acts 10:1-8). It is during one of Cornelius' times of prayer, alone before the face of the Lord that the Lord responds with His grace. Then we encounter Peter, who has himself escaped to the roof of a house to spend time alone with the Lord

---

1   It could be argued that there is a fourth sphere of worship in the Scriptures: national worship. The nation of Israel is often called together for worship in the Old Testament. However, for the purposes of this book and due to the passing of God's identification with a particular nation state, I do not address this sphere of worship here (or in this book).

(Acts 10:9). And as Peter seeks the Lord in prayer he is directed to go and minister to Cornelius, "this God-fearing man".

But maybe no greater argument needs to be made for the importance the Scriptures place upon secret worship than the very actions and words of our Savior. Jesus, the Son of God, who has constant communion with the Father, set-aside time for secret worship. As we are told in the Gospel of Mark, "And rising very early in the morning, while it was still dark, he departed and went out to a desolate place, and there he prayed" (Mark 1:35). If the Lord Jesus Christ deemed it important to spend time in secret worship, then we can be confident that it is an essential part of our life of worship as well! And Jesus makes this clear in the Sermon on the Mount. He assumes that followers of God will seek Him in prayer: "But *when* you pray, go into your room and shut the door and pray to your Father who is in secret" (Matt. 6:6, emphasis mine).

All of these passages and more show us that secret worship is the responsibility of the Christian. But Christians through the centuries have not just seen secret worship as their duty, but as their joy. Robert Murray M'Cheyne, a famous Scottish preacher from the nineteenth century, said this well in one of his sermons: "A believer longs after God—to come into His presence—to feel His love—to feel near to Him in secret—to feel in the crowd that he is nearer than all the creatures. Ah! dear brethren, have you ever tasted this blessedness? There is greater rest and solace to be found in the presence of God for one hour, than in an eternity of the presence of man."[2] The promise of secret

---

2   Robert Murray M'Cheyne, "The Good Way of Coming Before the Lord," (Sermon XIV). As printed in Andrew A. Bonar, *Memoir and Remains of the Rev. Robert Murray M'Cheyne* (Edinburgh: William Oliphant and Co.), p. 382.

worship, as in all of worship, is that we will be in the presence of our glorious God. There is no greater joy or blessing than that.

Second Sphere—Corporate Worship

Corporate worship is the second key sphere of worship in the Christian's life. If secret worship is a time in which we close the door in private and escape for a moment with God in the quietness of solitude, then corporate worship is at the other end of the continuum. This is the public and communal sphere of worship.

Not long ago, this book could have been written and only a brief sentence about the importance of corporate worship would have needed to be made. However, in the past few years the unthinkable has occurred: some Christians are actually arguing that the individual Christian has no need for corporate worship. How misguided and harmful this is!

There is a corporate nature to our faith. We are called the "flock" of Christ (Luke 12:32; John 10:16; Acts 20:28; 1 Pet. 5:2-3), the "bride" of Christ (Eph. 5; Rev. 19:7; Rev. 21:2, 9), and are told that we are being built into a "holy temple" in the Lord (Eph. 2:21). These are all corporate expressions. The greatest metaphor for the church in the New Testament is the language of the "body." We are the body of Christ. Yes, this speaks of our dependence upon the head, Christ Jesus, but it also proclaims our utter dependence upon one another. This is the very argument found in 1 Corinthians 12: "For just as the body is one and has many members, and all the members of the body, though many, are one body, so it is with Christ" (v. 12). We belong to one another and need one another. The writer of Hebrews reminds us to not forsake meeting together for this very reason (Heb. 10:25).

If we turn to Scripture, we see that whether they are at the foot of Mount Sinai, the temple, the synagogue, or the houses in Acts, God's people worship when they meet together. Our common bond is our union in Christ our Savior. Therefore, it is natural that when we gather together, we offer worship to our living God. Our lives are lived from Lord's Day to Lord's Day, as each week we long to "journey to the house of the Lord" to meet with our God and His people. Charles Spurgeon made these comments based upon Psalm 42:

> Debarred from *public* (emphasis mine) worship, David was heartsick. Ease he did not seek, honour he did not covet, but the enjoyment of communion with God was an urgent need of his soul; he viewed it not merely as the sweetest of all luxuries, but as an absolute necessity, like water to a stag. Like the parched traveller in the wilderness, whose skin bottle is empty, and who finds the wells dry, he must drink or die—he must have his God or faint. His *soul*, his very self, his deepest life, was insatiable for a sense of the divine presence. As the heart brays so his soul prays. Give him his God and he is as content as the poor deer which at length slakes its thirst and is perfectly happy; but deny him his Lord, and his heart heaves, his bosom palpitates, his whole frame is convulsed, like one who gasps for breath, or pants with long running.[3]

Third Sphere—Family Worship
The third sphere of worship is family worship, and this is the area that we will focus on in this book. Most evangelical Christians are aware of the importance of secret and corporate worship, but few have even heard of family worship. This sphere has fallen

---

3   Charles Spurgeon, *The Treasury of David,* Volume 1: Psalms 1-57 (Peabody, MA: Hendrickson Publishers, 1876), pp. 270-71.

on hard times! The next chapter will deal with the scriptural basis for family worship, but let us at this point at least make it clear that family worship is important for the Christian life. It should be something that the Christian family seeks to practice for the benefit of all in the home.

Family worship is that sphere of worship which incorporates those living under the same roof in a time of worship together. This may include a single mother with her children, three generations of a family, the immediate family and Uncle Bob, who is living in the spare room, or the traditional mom, dad, and 2.5 kids. Regardless of who makes up our family, it should be our desire and practice to gather together regularly for worship.

A Christian home is more than two or three Christians living in the same house. A few Christians living under the same roof does not make a place a Christian home any more than two or three bankers living in a house makes it a bank. A Christian home will seek to be centered upon Christ, and if it is centered upon Christ, then it will be filled with worship. As a Christian's life should be marked by setting time apart for secret worship, and just as our gathering together as the Christian community should be centered upon corporate worship, so should the home of a Christian family be marked by family worship. As Richard Baxter, that famous pastor of Kidderminster, said, "...prayer and praise are so necessary parts of God's service, that no family or person can be said in general to be devoted to serve God, that are not devoted to them."[4]

Worship is at the very center and core of what it means for us

---

4   Richard Baxter, *The Practical Works of Richard Baxter*, Volume 1 (Soli Deo Gloria Publications; Grand Rapids, MI: Soli Deo Gloria Publications, 2008), p. 419.

to be a Christian family. As Christian families, we want to see our families as worshiping families.

THREE SPHERES IN ONE LIFE

It is an over-used illustration—but I *am* a pastor, and few pastors have rejected an illustration because it's over-used—the illustration of the three-legged stool. If one leg is severed, then the stool does not stand. It may be propped up for a time, but it is wobbly and dangerous. The stool will eventually fall. It cannot bear up with only two legs. Similarly, the Christian life, as lived in worship, must function in all three of these spheres. A Christian will find it most beneficial to practice secret worship, corporate worship, *and* family worship. They are all important for our life in Christ. They each bear a necessary weight, and they all inform one another. When my secret worship is lacking or even non-existent, then my worship in the corporate community and family will be affected. When my attendance at corporate worship is sparse, then my secret worship and family worship will suffer as well. These three spheres of worship are related, informed, and encouraged by one another, because in each I am meeting with the Lord and benefiting from His grace. As I grow in my enjoyment of the Lord in my closet, so my enjoyment of Him in corporate worship will increase. As I hear the preached Word of God in corporate worship, this informs and stimulates my heart and mind in leading my own family in worship. As I worship God with my family, my affection and love for the Lord increases, which encourages my secret and corporate worship. They all inform one another. If I am starving in one area, then as I function in the other spheres I will find that I am malnourished there as well.

Each of these spheres of worship was appointed by God for

our good. They exist and function as a means by which He may pour out His ready grace upon us. It is an incredible gift. In the following chapters, we will consider why and how family worship can flourish in our lives; and as we grow in God's grace in this area, our worship in other areas will flourish as well. And in this way, it is grace upon grace.

CHAPTER 2

Give Me A Reason!
It's Our Joyful Responsbility!

As a pastor, it is always interesting on a Sunday morning to see someone making their way towards you with determination. This can either be a delightful or awful moment. One Sunday, at the end of the morning worship service, a woman came running up to me. Like most people in a similar situation, I was preparing myself for whatever was to come. Thankfully, she began smiling and shaking my hand. A few months before this particular Sunday, we had encouraged the congregation to begin worshiping with their families during the week at home. We put together a simple family worship outline and took opportunities to encourage the congregation to just try it. This mother had been very reluctant. She had some active, energetic young boys. As any of us parents of young boys can testify, there are days that swimming the English Channel during a raging thunderstorm with a fifty-pound weight tied around our ankles and sharks nipping at our toes seems like not only an enterprise at which we are more likely to succeed, but also a far more *enjoyable* prospect than getting our son(s) to sit still for more than three minutes. For this mother, the idea of reading the Scriptures and praying with her sons at home seemed undoable at best. However, after a few months, she was smiling and shaking my hand. Why? Because she said it had been one of the greatest blessings her home had enjoyed.

Is family worship always easy? No. How can it be with young, healthy, active boys at home? But leading our families in worship is a responsibility that is given to us. And make no mistake, it is a *joyful* responsibility that is given to us. The argument can be made that there is no direct command in the Bible to spend fifteen or twenty minutes a day worshiping with your family at home. You can search high and low and you won't find one. However, there are plenty of commands that in our homes we are to teach our children, read the Word, pray: in essence—worship. And these commands will be hard to obey without the kind of planning and consistency that family worship helps to provide.

A JOYFUL RESPONSIBILITY

The word "responsibility" might have tempted you to close the book. But, we shouldn't hesitate to use the word "responsibility." It may seem like a frightful word, but family worship is a joyful responsibility. It is joyful! Family worship is not drudgery. Is it scary? At times! Is it a struggle? Often! Is it worth it? Absolutely!

As Jonathan Edwards, that great preacher and writer of the First Great Awakening said, "Every Christian family ought to be as it were a little church."[1] Whose responsibility is it to

---

1   Jonathan Edwards, "Thoughts on the Revival of Religion in New England" in *The Works of Jonathan Edwards*, Volume 1 (Peabody, MA: Hendrickson Publishers, 1998), pp. 419-20.

encourage the home to be a "little church?" We could say that it is the husband and wife's joint responsibility. This is true in one sense, as they both should seek to encourage worship in their home and seek to support one another. In this way, both the husband and wife or father and mother share a general responsibility for family worship in the home—a responsibility not in the sense of something we *must* do, but something we *want* to do as Christians saved by such amazing grace. However, in a primary sense, spiritual leadership in the home is the husband's responsibility as one appointed to love and care for his wife. If there are children in the home, then it is primarily the father's responsibility as the head of the home to nurture those under his care by leading them in worship. If the father is absent, either physically or spiritually, then this joyful responsibility falls upon the mother. It would be nice if this were never the case, but it is far more a reality than we would like in our time. In such cases, the mother who remains will still desire to see the home filled with worship, and so she will pick up this mantle that ideally would not be hers.

BIBLICAL ENCOURAGEMENT

Maybe the earliest encouragement we see for family worship in the Bible is found in Genesis 18:19. God said that He chose Abraham "that he may command his children and his household after him to keep the way of the LORD…" How would Abraham have taught his children? There was no church. Abraham would have taught them at home. Throughout the time of the patriarchs, there was no one to gather with for worship other than those in their own family. And yet, the worship and truth of God continued to be passed on generation after generation through this family. With the Exodus from Egypt and the establishment of the nation came the formal ordinances of corporate worship. But even in the midst of giving His people the Law and establishing them as a nation of people for His sake, God underpins the importance of the Word being taught in the family. Deuteronomy 6:6-7 says, "And these words that I command you today shall be on your heart. You shall teach them diligently to your children, and shall talk of them when you sit in your house, and when you walk by the way, and when you lie down, and when you rise."

The Scriptures do not shy away from the distinct privilege and responsibility Christian parents have in raising their children to know, love, and enjoy God. It is clear in the commands of Scripture and the examples that are set. We are to have not only the mindset, but the follow-through that we see in parents such as Job, who are honored in Scripture. Here was a righteous man who took seriously the mandate to care for the spiritual state of his family. He would rise early and offer sacrifices and prayers for each of his children before the throne of God. The state of the souls of his children was daily upon his mind.

DARK SAYINGS OF OLD

Maybe nowhere is the importance of worship in our homes more clearly seen than in Psalm 78. This is a beautiful song about the Lord's care for the Israelite nation. The people of Asaph's generation have received the testimony of God's work and provision for the nation of Israel. And Asaph is reminding his generation that they must pass it on to the next generation.

The psalmist says, "I will open my mouth in a parable; I will utter dark sayings from of old" (v. 2). These are not dark sayings because they are hard to understand, but because they are to be looked into. What are these dark sayings that are to be carefully looked into? He gives us the answer in verse three: They are "things that we have heard and known, that our fathers have told us." He is describing what it would be a blessing to hear from the heads of Christian households today. We are not peddling some new "truths" or some unproven commodities. We are teaching that which has been handed down among believers for centuries. In reality, we are telling the story that has been told among faithful believers since the beginning of time. We are in a long line going all the way back to Adam: a line of faithful people who are telling the redemptive story—*the* story. This story is the one contained in the Scriptures; it is the factual story of God and His glorious deeds.

This psalm reminds us what we are to teach our families. When I think of my responsibility to care for my wife and children spiritually, I am not primarily concerned about passing on my subjective experiences. I am not concerned with passing on some fables or moral lessons. I am concerned with passing on the truth of our God—who He is and what He has done. As Christian parents, we have one of the greatest privileges in all of life: teaching our children to know God and His Word.

The Story Is *Our* Story

As you think about this, it may be helpful to remind yourself that we are not just telling some distant story about other people, but that we and our families are actors in this grand story of history. We need to continually remind our families and ourselves of this fact. And family worship provides a daily opportunity to do so. We are in a long line of saints from Adam to Noah to Jacob to Joseph to Nehemiah to John the Baptist to the Apostle Paul. As Christians, we want this story to continue through generations of our family to the glory of God. We have been recipients of this grace and want nothing more than to see this "good deposit" (2 Tim. 1:14) entrusted to us passed on to the next generation. There is no better daily way of encouraging this than to practice daily family worship.

I wonder if when you read the Scriptures you see yourself as a key figure in this redemptive story? I was reminded of this a few years ago when I was watching a children's Sunday School class at my church. One of the young six-year-old boys in the class was named Samuel (Sam). This particular Sunday, the class was looking at God's call of the prophet Samuel. The teacher asked if anyone knew the story. And little Sam's hand shot up. The teacher had barely called on Sam before he started rattling off the story. It was a joy to watch. This six-year-old boy was dramatically recalling the story with the loud call of God, "Samuel, Samuel." After about ten minutes of relaying all the events of that story, he finally stopped. The teacher asked him how he knew the story so well. And he replied, "It's about me!"

Do you see yourselves as key figures in the redemptive story? Not in the sense of little Sam, as he was a little off in his interpretation (adorably so), but do you understand that God continues to call and use us in His service for the extending of His Kingdom on earth—for His glory. Christian fathers, husbands, wives, and mothers, do you understand that you have this joyful responsibility?

The psalmist continues, "We will not hide them from their children, but tell them to the coming generation the glorious deeds of the LORD, and his might, and the wonders that he has done." (Ps. 78:4). Are we willing to make this same pledge? If we understand the importance of what has been handed down to us then we cannot keep it to ourselves. We must share it. Christian parents will want to ask the Lord to work through us so that this new generation might see His glorious deeds, His might, and the wonders that He has done—and that they might also "praise [His] glorious name" (1 Chron. 29:13). The church has historically seen family worship as one of the best and most helpful means of declaring this truth to the next generation and of giving glory to God in the current generation. Joel Beeke, in speaking on this topic at the 2011 Desiring God Conference for pastors, rightfully said, "The head of the family in leading his family in covenant faithfulness (family worship) to God is perhaps the most significant way God uses as a means of saving grace."

BLESSINGS BEYOND

However, it is not only the current generation and the next generation that family worship can impact to the glory and honor of God. The psalmist continues in verses five and six, "He established a testimony in Jacob and appointed a new law in Israel, which he commanded our fathers to teach to their children, that the next generation might know them, the children yet unborn, and arise and tell them to their children."

The psalmist is painting a picture in which one generation blesses the next generation, but the blessing doesn't stop there: it continues to flow down to those who follow. It is a cascade effect, with one generation impacting the next. I am familiar with this reality in a different way. I used to be an avid genealogist. It is fascinating to look back at your family tree and learn the names and birth places of your ancestors. However, what I found even more exciting in genealogical research were the stories that emerged from the pages of history about my family members: how just one "chance" meeting between two strangers resulted in a new branch in the family tree. My grandmother breaks the heel of her shoe and takes it into a shoe repair store, hands the shoe across the counter to a young, good-looking, Greek repair man, and before long, they are married. It is amazing how often that heel kept breaking after that first encounter! The introduction of one individual to another can change the course of our family tree and literally impact the next generation!

You and I also have a spiritual family tree. We do not know how many generations we may impact by sharing the gospel, the Scriptures, and our Lord with our children. Isn't the psalmist's hope in verse seven our greatest hope for our children? When I think about sharing the faith with my children, verse seven is often upon my mind: "So that they should set their hope in God and not forget the works of God, but keep his commandments." This must be our true heart's desire: that our children might set their hope in God and that they would teach their own children in turn. And that *they* would set their hope on God and teach *their* children and on and on it goes. If that is our desire, then family worship should have real appeal. How can it not?

A Call to Heads of the Home

In this psalm, Asaph does not lay this responsibility at the feet of the Levites or the priests, those who held public positions of spiritual leadership, but upon fathers. He says in verse five and following, "He established a testimony in Jacob and appointed a law in Israel, which He commanded our fathers to teach to our children." Religious education is the head of the home's responsibility. Thus, as I close this chapter, I want to speak directly to Christian fathers and husbands. In this day and age, as a whole, we fathers and husbands have generally neglected our charge. There are many Christian homes where the father or husband is spiritually or physically absent. And if that is the case, as we have said earlier and revisit later (see Chapter 8), we would encourage mothers to pick up this joyful responsibility. However, I know that many readers of this book will be Christian fathers, and you must especially hear this call. If a father is in the home, he must see himself as the pastor of this little congregation. He is to be the resident theologian of his home and is to serve as the pastor of the home, ministering to his wife and children. John Knox, the sixteenth-century father of Presbyterianism, said in a letter to refugees in Geneva, fathers, "you are bishops and kings; your wife, children, servants, and family are your bishopric and charge. Of you it shall be required how carefully and diligently you have always instructed them in God's true knowledge, how you have studied to plant virtue in them, and [to] repress vice. And therefore I say, you must make them partakers in reading, exhorting, and in making common prayers, which I would in every house were used once a day at least."[2]

Why do I say that fathers and husbands must especially wake up to this responsibility? I say this because, in an ideal world, fathers and husbands are leading their families in spiritual things. In creation, God ordained order and responsibility. Adam was made responsible for Eve. The manner in which God creates her by taking a rib from Adam serves as a tangible sign of this. She is equal to him in stature and dignity, but he is responsible for her. She is under his care and his protection. Have you ever wondered why the sin in the Garden of Eden is referred to in the Scriptures as Adam's sin? It was Eve who "saw that the tree was good for food, and that it was a delight to the eyes." It was Eve who first "took of its fruit and ate." Only after she had

---

2   John Knox, "A Letter of Wholesome Counsel to His Brethren in Scotland 1556" in *Selected Writings of John Knox: Public Epistles, Treatises, and Expositions to the Year 1559*.(Dallas, TX: Presbyterian Heritage Publications, 1995.)

taken a bite did "she also [give] some to her husband who was with her, and he ate" (Gen. 3:6). And yet the Scriptures call it Adam's sin (Hosea 6:7; Rom. 5:14). Why? Because Adam was responsible for Eve. Her guilt is not his. But he is responsible for her. Even after the Fall, the husband and wife relationship has not changed in this regard. The husband is still responsible for the spiritual state of his wife and his children. They are under his care. Therefore, the Christian husband will seek to lead his wife, and the Christian father will seek to lead his children in the pursuit of God.

In 1 Timothy 5:8, Paul tells his young protégé, "But if anyone does not provide for his relatives, and especially for members of his household, he has denied the faith and is worse than an unbeliever." Paul is speaking about the responsibility that a head of the home has to those within it. This man's position is not one of indulgence, but of provision. His responsibility is great. He is to provide for those under his care. And this provision is not only for their physical needs. Many Christian fathers and husbands think that they are fulfilling their God-given duty because they are providing for the material needs of their family. This is not enough! If our wives and children were only material bodies, then it would make sense to provide solely for their material needs. But they are not just bodies; they have eternal souls. Their spiritual well-being must also be cared for.

Ephesians 5-6 makes this very point regarding husbands and fathers. The husband is the head of his wife as Christ is the head of the church. The question is never *whether* the husband is the head of his wife. The only question is whether he is *functioning* as a godly head of his wife. He is to point her to Christ. In this same passage Paul commissions fathers to care for their children: "Fathers, do not provoke your children to anger, but bring them up in the discipline and instruction of the Lord" (Eph. 6:4). We are to disciple and instruct those who are in our care. Surely we do this by leading them to church on Sunday and answering their questions about God before bed. But this is not sufficient. As Donald Whitney, a current professor at Southern Baptist Theological Seminary, said about this text, "Without some regularity and structure and purpose, it is one of those things that we assume we are doing but never actually do. Consistent, father-led family worship is one of the best, steadiest, and most easily measurable ways to bring up children in the Lord's discipline and instruction."[3] If we neglect this opportunity to worship together, then we are missing what should be at the very center of our family life.

Husbands and fathers, God has given you the pleasure, as the head of the home, to serve as His under-shepherd in caring for this little flock. It is time that we take up our staff and tend the sheep the Lord has blessed us with. It is hard, if not impossible, to adequately care for His sheep, our family, if we are neglecting worship in our home. Maybe this is the first time that you have considered family worship, or maybe it has been something you have started and stopped. In either case, this is the time to pick it up. Family worship can be one of the most beneficial and satisfying aspects of you and your family's life in Christ. How good it is to lead your family before God and reencounter each day His abundant grace! Is it always easy? No. But is it our joyful responsibility? Yes. So let us strive to lead our

---

3   Donald S. Whitney, *Family Worship: In the Bible, in History, and in Your Home* (Distributed by The Center for Biblical Spirituality, Shepherdsville, KY, 2005), p. 7.

families well, wholly leaning upon Christ. Let us be men who love our Lord well by loving our families well. And let us love our families well by caring for their souls. And let us care for their souls by leading our wives and children in worship. What a delight you will find it to be! We close this chapter with the encouragement of Douglas Kelly, a noted Reformed theologian and professor:

> A reverent reading of Old and New Testament will leave us with this unmistakable conclusion: family religion, which depends not a little on the household head daily leading the family before God in worship, is one of the most powerful structures that the covenant-keeping God has given for the expansion of redemption through the generations, so that countless multitudes may be brought into communion with and worship the One who is worthy "to receive glory and honor and power: for thou has created all things, and for thy pleasure they are and were created" (Rev. 4:11).[4]

As we think about the biblical encouragement and joyful responsibility we have to worship God in our homes, we realize that our primary reason for engaging in family worship is the glory of God. God is honored and glorified as a Christian family gathers to commune with Him, receive from Him, and give praise, adoration, and thanksgiving to Him. Family worship is a living banner that speaks louder than any sign over our mantlepiece or any engraving on the wall which loudly proclaims, "As for me and my house, we will serve the LORD" (Josh. 24:15).

---

4 Douglas F. Kelly, "Family Worship: Biblical, Reformed, and Viable for Today," in *Worship in the Presence of God*, eds. David Lachman and Frank J. Smith (Greenville, SC: Greenville Seminary Press, 1992), pp. 110-11.

CHAPTER 3

How About Some Other Practical Reasons?

Primarily, we want to engage in family worship because it honors and glorifies God. But there are many other benefits to family worship which accompany our practice of it. Here, we will consider just a few of these.

CENTERS HOME

Family worship has the wonderful effect of centering our homes upon Christ. It is difficult to make the argument that we are a Christian family and that God is the center of our lives when our homes are centered upon something else. All of us can benefit from thinking about what our home is centered upon. If most of us are honest, it is probably not Christ. We love Christ, we are Christians, and we pray for our families every day. But our homes are not centered upon Christ. There are so many good and enjoyable things in life that these easily take center stage without us even noticing.

Daily family worship provides a continual reminder that we are worshipers of Christ. It has the added benefit of shaping the home around this worship. A family that reads the Bible, prays together, and sings praise to God will begin to have its actions, thoughts, and words shaped by this daily event. Isn't this the kind of home that we want? As a young parent, I can't tell you how many empty nesters have commented to me, "Enjoy your children while you have them, because before you know it they will be on their own." Before our children leave our home, by God's grace, I want them to have experienced a home that is filled with worship. As parents, we want our children leaving the home thankful for many things. It is good that we take them to soccer games and curl up on the couch to watch a television show together. My kids and I love to snuggle on the couch, watch Julia Child cook, and try to imitate her voice. But I don't want that memory to be the dominant one in their minds because those are the kinds of events which dominated our life together.

When our children leave the home, what will they say was the center of the family's life together? Do we want them *primarily* thankful for parents who watched television with them and attended all their games? Or do we desire that our children leave the home with an understanding that worship is the center of who we are and what we do and that Christ is what was most cherished? I think all of us would say that our desire, by God's grace, is that our children might say one day, "Our parents were quirky, had many faults, and were by no means perfect. But we know that they loved the Lord, worshiped Him, and were determined to share Christ's love with us."

ENCOURAGES OUR CHILDREN IN CHRIST
Family worship encourages our children in the things of Christ. They will see from Mom and Dad that worship is not just something they do on Sunday mornings. It is something that is

at the very core of their being and is the most important thing we do. We are not raising them to be just moral and competent people, but worshipers of God.

As one Christian mother remarked to me, it is easy to settle into the mindset that the goal in raising children is to prepare them to be mature individuals, who when they leave to go out into the world, are competent and ready for the world. But that isn't enough. You and I, as Christian parents, can't be content with something so limited and small. As *Christian* parents, our goal in raising our children is not to prepare them for going out into the world as fully functioning adults. Our goal, as Christian parents, is to prepare our children for eternity! This has to be the greatest desire of any Christian parent. Everything else in our children's life and world is a distant second in importance. For we know that, in the end, it is their faith in Christ and living for Him that matters. We can't make this happen. I surely can't guarantee it. But I do know that family worship directs our children to seek Christ daily, and that is the very best I can give them. I don't think it is an overstatement to say that the single greatest encouragement we can give to our children unto their salvation is daily family worship. If that isn't enough reason to start, I don't know what could be.

ENCOURAGES CHRISTIAN CHARACTER

The home may be the hardest place to live out our Christian lives. There is a reason that Paul addresses each member of the Christian family in the household passages of Ephesians 5–6 and Colossians 3. It is a sad reality that we often manifest the character of Christ and the graces of the Spirit more consistently at church, in the workplace, and in the community then we do in our own homes. Some would say this speaks of our hypocrisy as Christians, but it is something much more profound than that! We often see our home as a refuge from the world and we "let our hair down" when we enter the door. We change into comfortable clothes and relax. In many ways, we often do this spiritually as well when we come home. Our safeguards and defenses are let down. We allow the familiarity and comfortableness to lull us to sleep and we lose our attentiveness in guarding against sin and pursuing righteousness.

It is reported that most traffic accidents happen within a mile of a person's home. Why? One factor is that we drive near our home more often than anywhere else. However, this is not the only factor. It is also because as we get closer to home, we become more comfortable and lose our alertness. If there is somewhere that I must especially be on guard against sin, the flesh, and our adversary, it is at home. Casualness and familiarity is a ready playing field for sin. And family worship serves as a daily reminder that we must see ourselves in relation to Christ at home even as we do outside the home. In truth, our Christian character or lack thereof is probably more evidenced by the way we live within the confines and comfortableness of our home and family than anywhere else.

ENCOURAGES PEACE IN THE HOME

We are sinners living under the same roof in tight quarters. That is a recipe for disaster, or at least pain! We know our family members and we know them well. It is also true that they know us and know us well! They have seen moments in which our pride gets stung, our selfishness is exerted, our anger flares, or our slothfulness takes hold. And we have seen it in them. As we all know, our sins never only affect us. They also affect others, especially those with whom we are closest. Those we love the most have often caused us the greatest amount of pain, and we them. This is just the reality of love and families. The greater our love, the greater possibility there is to hurt one another. And it is usually pain over the course of time that takes the largest toll on a family.

As a pastor, I have seen very few marriages end in divorce because of one act of adultery or some other "notorious" sin. Rather, most divorces occur because of built-up pain, a lack of forgiveness, grudges, etc., which have accumulated over time. Family worship aids a family to confront their own sin and its effect upon each other. As an example, it is awfully hard for a father to lead his family in worship when he has just yelled at his wife. If he is going to lead his family before the throne of grace, he will first have to ask for forgiveness from his wife. And she will find that it is hard to worship unless she willingly forgives him. This couple's children will observe and learn from this. They will be encouraged to pursue peace and forgiveness as they see their father and mother model it. And if they are struggling with each other or with their parents, then family worship provides the opportunity for the entire family to go before God in confession and repentance, and to receive His grace and comfort. You will be amazed by the impact that family worship can have upon the peace of your home.

A wife who was struggling with criticalness and judging her husband relayed to me that she found family worship was one of the key components in her fighting this sin. This couple turned their prayer time in family worship to prayers of thanksgiving for life, God's goodness, and one another. And as the weeks went by, she discovered that she was more thankful and her marriage enjoyed more peace. Christ, that great Prince of

Peace, often encourages peace in the Christian home through family worship.

BINDS THE FAMILY TOGETHER

In our fast-moving and ever-busy society, there are few things that a family does daily together. Even eating a meal together these days seems like a feat. What if your family came together daily for worship? This activity would become the most important and central aspect of your family's life. Your entire family would come to the realization that no matter what else we do or don't do, the most important thing that marks us as a family is that we are a worshiping family, enjoying Christ and seeking to follow Him. And that bond is an eternal bond that strengthens the family in all its other endeavors. A father recently remarked to me, "It has been so much fun listening to my daughter pray in family worship. Her requests have not only surprised me, but informed me of what she is wrestling with." As you worship together, you will know each other better and love each other more fully.

PROVIDES COMMON KNOWLEDGE

As you daily read the Scriptures together as a family, you will grow in your knowledge of the Bible. And you will be growing together as a family! Most of our churches have moved into the practice of having age-defined Sunday school classes, fellowship groups, etc. There may be some positives to this, but one of the negatives is that the elementary school children are learning something different from what their parents are learning, which is different from what their teenage siblings are learning. The car ride home from church or the Sunday afternoon conversation is stymied. However, as you read the Scriptures together in family worship, everyone is growing together in a common knowledge. It is a wonderful thing to learn and grow together. Your conversations around the dinner table or in the car will change dramatically as you have a common knowledge from which to converse.

EQUIPS OUR CHILDREN FOR CORPORATE WORSHIP

Family worship provides the added benefit of training our children for corporate worship. As they sit and listen to the Word of God, hear prayers, or sing hymns, the same elements found in corporate worship at church will take on a new meaning. The value of this cannot be overestimated. As our children learn to pray at home, they will participate more readily in corporate prayer at church. As they learn the hymns or songs of the faith in family worship, the same hymns and songs will resonate with them on Sunday mornings.

A number of years ago we decided to teach our daughter the Lord's Prayer during our family worship. Her little three-year-old mind and tongue worked at it weekly. One Sunday morning, I was leading worship in our congregation and in that particular service we were praying the Lord's Prayer. I guess that we had never prayed it in our service during the time in which I was teaching my daughter to memorize it. I will never forget looking out at the congregation, and my eyes fell upon her. When the congregation began praying the Lord's Prayer, her little head raised up and she began to smile. And then she began to look at all the people around her who were reciting this prayer that she knew. She was beaming from ear to ear. She knew this prayer!

REINFORCES SPIRITUAL HEADSHIP

Family worship reinforces the biblical framework of the family as the family looks to the father (or the mother if she is single) as the head of the home and spiritual leader. As the father leads his children and wife before God's throne and disciples them in the things of Christ, they will increasingly look to him for spiritual leadership. This has the added benefit of reinforcing with the father/husband the spiritual mantle that is upon his shoulders. He has quite a responsibility before the Lord, and daily family worship will help him to focus upon this responsibility. I am surprised by how easy it is to go through a day, get caught up in its busyness, and not think about the souls of my wife and children. It is also easy, as too many of us can confess, to forget to be intentional in ministering to our family each day. As fathers and husbands, family worship helps to orient our minds and time to that which is most important in our roles as husband and father. It also has the benefit of helping us to see our inadequacy for this charge. We will find ourselves becoming more dependent upon God, seeking Him in prayer, asking for His grace, and submitting to His headship. And that is prerequisite to leading our families well.

Provides Systematic Discipleship

As a pastor, I often have parents and sometimes spouses approach me with a question about how to minister to their children or spouse in a specific area. Usually they are concerned about a particular sin or struggle in their children's or spouse's life. For example, a husband may seek to know how to aid his wife in dealing with anxiousness or selfishness. A mother may seek wisdom in how to rightly instruct her son not to tell lies. In this way, we serve as firefighters, rushing to extinguish this issue or that. At times this is needed, but it should not be our only course of action. As a spouse or parent, I must not only be concerned about "remedies," but preventative care for my loved ones. One of the best avenues for preventative care—and, as far as that goes, remedies as well—will be found in the systematic discipleship provided in family worship. We often are so busy concerning ourselves with quick fixes that we ignore the benefits received by hearing the whole counsel of God in our homes over time. Daily family worship will provide a strong foundation that is built upon hearing the Word daily, praying daily, and giving thanks daily. It takes time to build a strong house. If we are just running from shaky wall to shaky wall to hammer a nail in here and a nail in there, the result is an unsteady home. Family worship is a great aid in establishing a steady home.

This chapter has reviewed several beneficial and practical effects of family worship. Any one of these might be reason enough to begin family worship, but all together they show how important this activity really is. And this is just a taste of the benefits. As you start family worship in your home, you will find God's grace manifested to you and your family in ways that you did not consider. Some of us may become discouraged that we don't immediately see some of the benefits mentioned in this book or perhaps what we expected; but I encourage you to persist. What Paul said to the Galatians could easily be said to those who begin family worship: "Let us not grow weary of doing good, for in due season we will reap, if we do not give up" (Gal. 6:9). God knows what you and your family need, and by His grace He will supply it in due time. This you can be assured of.

Now that we have considered the "why's" of family worship, we will turn to the "what"—what does family worship look like? Chapter four describes the basic components of family worship in more detail.

CHAPTER 4

Now What? What Do I Do?

_____

Family worship may not be familiar to many of us. Even if we agree that family worship is important, we may not know what to do. Below we will consider some of the cardinal elements of family worship, including reading God's Word, praying, and singing. We will also consider other activities that could be fruitful parts of our worship times together.

WORSHIP

Family worship is worship. That may sound like a silly statement, but it is a crucial starting point for our family worship in the home. The negative way of saying the same thing is that family worship is not entertainment, just plain family time, or even reading a good Christian children's book together. There is a place for all these things in the home, but they are not family worship. Reading from a good Christian book can be very helpful and a blessing to the entire family, but this should not be substituted for family worship. Likewise, every family should set aside time to just enjoy each other. This may mean gathering together to play games, watch a movie, or discuss the day's events, but none of these things is family worship. Family worship is, first and foremost, worship. Therefore, as we approach it we must remind ourselves what worship is.

What is the act of worship? Above all else, worship is our communing with the one true and living God. Or, better stated, His communing with us. In that communing, the primary thing that happens is our meeting with Him. This is the true delight of worship. We, a sinful people, saved by grace, have the great joy of being with Him. It is also true that we are giving to Him, and He is giving to us. We give adoration, praise, and thanksgiving to Him, all to His honor and glory. And He gives us His grace and blessing. He ministers to us by binding our wounds, encouraging us in righteousness, exhorting us to live for Him, teaching us, assuring us of our salvation, reminding us of His promises, and pouring out His love upon us. Therefore, it is primarily in worship that we are discipled and grow in Christ.

God chooses to receive our adoration, praise, and thanksgiving in the same way that He chooses to give us His grace and blessing. He uses the same means or elements in both giving and receiving. They are appointed by Him. And they are the same elements we find in corporate worship: prayer, Scripture, and singing (along with the sacraments, which are appropriate only in corporate worship). A family that prays together, reads the Bible together, and sings together is a family which is placing itself in the way of God's grace. Spurgeon, commenting on family worship, asserts: "I agree with Matthew Henry when he says, 'They that pray in the family do well; they that pray and read the Scriptures do better; but they that pray, and read, and sing do best of all.' There is a completeness in that kind of family worship which is meant to be desired."[1]

Therefore, as we approach family worship, regardless of what we do or don't do, the essential elements are reading the Scriptures, praying, and singing. These are the primary means or instruments by which God meets with us by His Spirit, we praise Him, and He showers His grace upon us.

THE SCRIPTURES

God has given us His Word. As we come to family worship, it is easy to replace the reading and hearing of the Word of God with a good Christian children's book or a moral story from which our children can learn. This can be quite helpful, but not in the place of the Word of God. God has given His Word to His people. We have no greater gift to give our children than the Word of God. *The Westminster Shorter Catechism* has a beautiful description of what the Scriptures contain. Westminster Shorter Catechism Question Three asks, "What do the Scriptures principally teach?" Its answer is, "The Scriptures principally teach what man is to believe concerning God, and what duty God requires of man."

God has chosen to work through His Word. It is the seed that is scattered and produces fruit (Mark 4:1-20). It is "breathed out by God and profitable for teaching, for reproof, for correction, and for training in righteousness" (2 Tim 3:16). It is true and without error. It is living and active (Heb. 4:12). In these pages is life, light, truth, and the promise of peace and eternal joy. Why would we ever seek to give our children something less? If

---

1   Charles Spurgeon, "The Happy Duty of Daily Praise," *Metropolitan Tabernacle Pulpit,* Volume 32 (London: Passmore and Alabaster, 1886; reprint, Pasadena, TX: Pilgrim Publications, 1986), p. 289.

the Scriptures teach the truth of God and what He desires from us, which they do, then they must have central place in our worship together. God has chosen to minister to His people by His Word.

Some parents are reluctant to read the Bible to their children for fear that their children cannot understand the Bible, and so they decide to read something else with them while they are young. Though these parents are trying to be sensitive to their children, they are underestimating the wisdom of God. God can be trusted to know what is best in the nurturing of our children, and we should trust in the efficacy of His Word. You may need to take time to explain the reading of the Scripture to your children, or you may need to read very small sections, but we shouldn't abandon the reading of the Scriptures altogether. We too often underestimate the power of the Word of God. And we too often underestimate our children.

Right now, my son is four years old and my daughter is seven years old. We read the Scriptures together during our family worship. Neither one of them understands everything we read, but there are things that grip them. I do my best to explain the verses to them and ask questions to help them engage the text and think through it. More often than not, they ask my wife and I all kinds of questions about the passage. Recently, we have been reading through the Gospel of John. When we came to John 8, where Christ says, "I am the light of the world," my children were immediately engaged. They wanted to know what it meant that Jesus was the light.

I thought they understood until my son started pointing at the chandelier and asking, "Is that Jesus?" "No, son." And then he pointed at the lamp on the table, "Is that Jesus?" "No, son, that isn't Jesus either." "Oh," He says, "That must be Jesus," as he pointed at the kitchen light. Though they didn't understand what it means that Jesus is the light that night, despite all my attempts, this discussion continued for another week. The questions kept coming because they wanted to talk about it more. It became our topic of conversation on car rides and as we were walking down the grocery store aisles. And a week later my children were clearly articulating the truth that Jesus is the light. It is fascinating that even today my son is enamored with this facet of the person of Christ.

In our family, we always take small portions of text or narratives which allow them to engage the text, because they are so young. I don't know what work the Spirit is doing in them by His Word, but I do know that the Word of God as it goes out does not return void; it accomplishes that which God purposes (Isa. 55:11). We cannot say this about any other word or book. God's Word will accomplish His purposes! And I must trust in it and minister to my family by it. It is the Word of God that will stand forever (Isa. 40:8), and this is what we should want planted in the hearts of our family. Although the fruit might not be immediately apparent, we can trust that over time God will use the teaching of His Word in the lives of our children, even as He uses it in our own lives.

How much Scripture should a family read together? A good place to start might be to read a chapter a day. With small children, I would recommend that you read less than a chapter. But do read it aloud. It is not just the teaching of God's Word that is effectual, but the reading of it. And so we want to make sure that we read aloud the Word of God in our home. I encourage mothers, fathers, and husbands to practice reading the Scriptures aloud. As we read aloud, we are interpreting the Scriptures for those around us. The way we inflect a word or place emphasis upon another word will affect their understanding of the passage. Therefore, when we read we will want to approach the reading of God's Word with care. It may be helpful to listen to some masterful readers of the Scriptures such as Max McLean or some of your favorite preachers as they read the text they are going to preach. The act of reading is also beneficial for the reader: it will prepare you for the lesson that evening and allow you to meditate upon the passage before leading family members through it.

In addition to reading God's Word, it is also important to try and help your family understand the passage. Before reading the text, give a sentence or two introduction, so that they know the context of the passage. This may take a little bit of preparation, but the time spent will pay huge dividends. After reading the text, it is always helpful to give a brief interpretation or to ask questions that lead your children to recite the text back to you. You may also want to take some time to apply the text and to help your children understand the application that should flow from this reading. It doesn't have to be profound or original; this shouldn't be a concern. Your only concern should be helping all the members of your family to understand the truth of the Scripture and live it out in their daily lives. Some of us may not be ready to teach our wife/children, and that is fine! Take your time. It is something to endeavor towards. However, do not let that fear stop you from reading the Word of God with your family.

As we read the Bible in family worship, we want to allow the "whole counsel of God" (Acts 20:27) to influence our family.

Therefore, the best regular approach in family worship is to read systematically through one book of the Bible at a time. This does not always need to be the case, and at times you may select certain passages which minister to the issues your family is currently facing or take a series of chapters such as the Joseph account in Genesis. However, in general, it is best to regularly read through an entire book. It is difficult for adults, let alone children, to remember the context of 1 Samuel 22 when we last read from 1 Samuel two months ago! The Bible is one book, but it is also 66 books. And therefore we should approach each book as such. Read through the entire Gospel of Mark and then turn to another book like Joel and begin reading through it. This also prevents anyone from "cherry-picking" favorite Scriptures or "brow-beating" fellow family members by reading what one individual thinks the rest need to hear. Over time, God will minister to all your family needs as you read through "the whole counsel of God." A "shotgun" approach to Scripture, picking this passage over here today and that passage over there tomorrow, will be less fruitful in the long run.

During our family worship, before I begin reading the Scriptures, I usually ask my youngest, "What book of the Bible are we in?" The other night he rightly answered, "John." I replied, "Last night we finished John chapter 5, what chapter are we beginning tonight?" My son yelled out, "Chapter 6." He then said, "Daddy, what happens when we have finally read through the entire Bible?" My answer, "We get to read through it again!" Wouldn't it be a blessing to be able to read through the entire Bible multiple times as a family while our children were still at home? But be careful; don't move too fast! It is better to read slowly and marinate in the passages than to quickly read large portions of Scripture and to have your family become overwhelmed or confused by attempting to read too much at once. A family that reads carefully through entire books will begin to see the entire Bible unfold; connections will be seen from the Book of Romans to Isaiah or the Psalms to the Gospel of Matthew. And what benefits there are to hiding the Word of God in the hearts of our family members like this!

I had a young girl in Sunday School class who kept answering all the questions I was asking during a particular lesson. But it was how she was answering the questions that struck me. She was quoting passages from 1 John. Or if it wasn't a direct quote, they were paraphrases of different verses from the book—every answer. And I asked her, "How do you know these answers?" She gave me an incredulous reply, "These are easy, they are in the Bible." After class, I asked her father how she knew these things. He said they had been reading through 1 John during family worship and she loved the book. It seems that she had begun memorizing it. The Word of God was hidden in the heart of a child.

PRAYER

Another necessary element of our family worship is prayer. There are few things sweeter than a family that prays together. During family worship, you may pray one prayer or multiple prayers. Encourage your family to spend time in adoration, confession, intercession, and thanksgiving. These are all types of prayers that should be familiar to your family over the course of time. Some nights you may pray each. Other nights you may choose to just pray prayers of intercession for sick church members or neighbors who do not know Christ. If you are not sure how to lead your family in prayer, then picking up a good old resource such as Matthew Henry's *A Method for Prayer* or Isaac Watts' *A Guide to Prayer*, or something more recent such as Paul Miller's *A Praying Life* or Eric Alexander's *Prayer: A Biblical Perspective*, will be very helpful. Your prayer time does not need to be long or overly complex, especially if you have small children. You may elect to have different family members pray different prayers or to lead the prayer time itself. This is also an opportunity to pray for one another and solicit prayer requests from your family members. It is a blessing to the whole family when you know how to pray for one another during the day and throughout the week. It is also a blessing to others. Because my children are young, we usually ask them to pray for certain individuals in the church or our family. It is a blessing to see my daughter walk up to "Mr. Jones" at church and ask how his leg is doing. She has a vested interest: she has been praying for his leg!

Song

For the vast majority of families, this is initially the most awkward element of family worship. Most of us are not that excited about the voices we have been blessed with! And those around us aren't real sure they are a blessing either! And it is impossible to hide your voice when there are only two, three, four, or five people in the room. But don't let the initial awkwardness and off-key notes deter you from singing praise together as a family. I thought we were decent at singing until we bought a new puppy. The first night we did family worship in the same room as him, he began to howl. I thought it was just the newness of the noise. But the following night he did the same thing. If we can continue to sing, though we make dogs cry out in pain, you can too!

It is always helpful if an individual in the family is musically inclined and can play the piano or another instrument in accompaniment, but most of us do not have that luxury. Therefore, you must learn to sing a cappella, or you can visit one of the helpful websites which provide selectable songs and hymns that your family can sing along with (see Appendix C). Your family may not sound like the "Three Tenors," but sing with your full voices. The Scriptures say that we are to make "a joyful noise to the Lord" (Ps. 95:1-2; 98:4-6; 100:1). And for some of us, that is just what it is, joyful *noise.* But it is still pleasing to God (granted, Christ is interceding for us!).

I would encourage you to have a good hymnal from which to sing. Ideally, every person in the family or every two people should have a hymnal to use. For young children, it is helpful to have a hymnal placed before them as they sit on their parent's lap and for their parent to move their finger along the page with the music. Children may not be able to read the words or the music, but they will begin to understand that everyone is singing from the hymnal. And they will begin to resonate with the music and look forward to singing. When my daughter was three, she loved getting the hymnal down from the shelf each night. If we sat down and the hymnal was not there, she would run and get it. She loved the hymnal. She couldn't sing the words of any of the hymns yet, but that didn't stop her from joining her voice with ours. She was making a joyful noise. And that had the added benefit of her joining in singing during corporate worship at church.

My children are of the age now that they love to sing faithful children's songs, so that is what we do. My son requests "Deep and Wide" every night we do family worship. And he insists that we all do the motions! My daughter loves the "B-I-B-L-E." And we all have to yell "Bible" at the end or it is requested again. Some of your families may enjoy singing along with a digital recording. A family I know well plays their kids' favorite worship songs from their iPods. Each child gets a night to pick a song, and the family joins in.

You may want to begin with hymns or songs which everyone in the family knows. And then, once the family begins to feel a little more comfortable with singing, you can begin introducing new hymns and songs to sing. As you introduce new hymns or songs into your family worship setting, you may think about singing one new hymn or song nightly for a few weeks until your family knows it. If you introduce one new hymn to your family a month and just focus on singing that hymn, over the course of ten years they will have learned one-hundred-and-twenty hymns. Regardless of how many hymns or songs we sing, we must always make sure that the hymns and songs we sing are theologically rich and true according to God's Word. We are those who are to worship in "Spirit and in truth" (John 4:24).

As we think about singing in family worship, we should also consider singing the Psalms from the Old Testament. This is the "song book" of the Scriptures. Singing the Psalms is foreign to many of us. Much of the church over the last hundred years has abandoned the singing of the Psalms, but there are few more rewarding pursuits. There are many good Psalters available today (see Appendix C). As we sing the Psalms in our family worship, we are singing God's Word back to Him. And we have the added benefit of hiding the Word of God in our hearts through song. Music is often the best way to memorize, and over time you will find that by singing the Psalms you and your children have memorized entire psalms of the Old Testament. A good companion to the hymnal on your shelf at home is the Psalter. The tunes may not be familiar, but in this day and age there are many resources to help us in this area. A quick search on the internet will produce a downloadable audio file of the tune, and there are a number of good music albums with psalm singing.

ADDITIONAL ELEMENTS

There are other elements of worship which we can incorporate into our times of family worship. I will mention these more briefly, but each may be important supplements to reading Scripture, praying, and singing.

Scripture Memory: We always want to hide the Word of God in our hearts. As a family, this is a wonderful exercise to do together, taking a verse a week to memorize with each other. Even small children can memorize the Word of God. You will be surprised at what a three- or four-year-old can memorize. They are usually better at it than their parents! If your family memorized one verse every two weeks for fifteen years, your children (and you!) will have memorized 390 verses! Now that is planting the Word of God in the hearts of our children! Over time, you may even lead your children through the exercise of memorizing a whole book. Start with a small book such as 2 John and by encouragement they will begin to memorize larger books. The blessing of memorization is that it affords a person the opportunity to meditate upon the Word of God wherever they are and whatever their circumstances: verses will come to mind in the midst of a trial and provide comfort, a favorite passage will occupy our minds as we drive down the road, or a child may be pricked in conscience as they face a decision.

The benefits of Scripture memorization far outweigh any struggle it is for us to memorize.

Scripture memorization can be accomplished in various ways. Some families may find it helpful to write the verses together or to fill in the missing words of a verse you have already written on a dry erase board. Others may prefer to use flashcards. Still others may enjoy memorizing Scripture to song. There are a lot of different ways to memorize. Be creative and fun with your memorization methods. And don't fall into a rut! Try various methods as some of your family members may benefit from one method more than another.

In a church I served, it was our practice to have the elders interview children for membership when their parents believed they had come to faith and were ready to be admitted to the Lord's Table. On one occasion, we interviewed a ten-year-old young lady who had been led in family worship by her single father for years. Part of their family worship consisted of memorizing passages of Scripture. She eventually moved on to memorizing whole books. During our interview of her, we were asking different questions. At one point in the interview we asked her a question and she began quoting passages from Habakkuk. I have never interviewed an adult for membership, let alone a child, who has answered questions with quotations from Habakkuk! But this young lady did, because it was part of her. She had memorized this book and it had become part of her vocabulary and thought.

Catechism: Catechizing is a lost discipline in the evangelical church today, and we are suffering as a result. This is a tried and proven method that has been used across Christian traditions. It is a means of instilling within our hearts and minds the doctrine and theology of the Scriptures. Catechism uses a question-answer format. A theological question is asked and the teaching of the Scriptures on that subject is given in the reply. For example, maybe the most famous catechism question is the first question of the *Westminster Shorter Catechism*, which asks, "What is the chief end of man?" The answer is, "The chief end of man is to glorify God and enjoy Him forever." This is a helpful, biblical, and theologically rich explanation for the reason man exists. Scripture memory allows us to quote what this or that verse says on prayer, but it is difficult to give a thorough and concise definition of prayer by quoting one verse or even two. A catechism simply takes the teaching of the Scriptures on an entire subject and provides a concise statement on that teaching.

As we disciple our children, it is crucial that we not only hide the Word of God in their hearts, but also help them to understand the theology and doctrines of the Scriptures. They need a theological framework, derived from the Scriptures, by which they can think and act. And catechizing serves this very purpose. Just listen to this first question and answer of the *Heidelberg Catechism*: "Question: What is thy only comfort in life and death? Answer: That I with body and soul, both in life and death, am not my own, but belong unto my faithful Savior Jesus Christ; who, with his precious blood, has fully satisfied for all my sins, and delivered me from all the power of the devil; and so preserves me that without the will of my heavenly Father, not a hair can fall from my head; yea, that all things must be subservient to my salvation, and therefore, by his Holy Spirit, He also assures me of eternal life, and makes me sincerely willing and ready, henceforth, to live unto him." What a blessing it would be to have this beautiful statement in the minds of our children!

Confessions of Faith: A related element that can be practiced in family worship is confession from a confession of faith or ancient creed of the church. As an example, the *Apostle's Creed* and *Nicene Creed* are statements that would be appropriate to recite together during family worship. These are creeds which articulate the essential truths of the Christian faith. As we confess our faith from a creed such as the *Apostle's Creed*, we are joining our voices with Christians throughout the centuries and today who have believed in the one true God. We are professing a common faith and confessing that this is the God in whom we believe. Regardless of whether or not one chooses to use a confession of faith during family worship, the memorization of these two creeds is a useful part of the instruction and discipleship our children receive. Most hymnals will include these two creeds and possibly a catechism. In addition, I have included the *Apostle's Creed* and *Nicene Creed* in the appendix of this book for your use.

Responsive Readings: Responsive readings can be an aid in involving the whole family in the reading of Scripture. Children especially enjoy responsive readings. Many hymnals provide responsive readings from the Psalms in the back of the hymnal. A parent could also create a responsive reading from the Scriptures for the family to read. There are some samples in the appendix of this book to help you get started.

Other Books: We may add reading from other helpful books. However, this should only supplement our reading of the Scriptures in family worship. Reading a passage from a Christian classic such as *Pilgrim's Progress* or a good Christian biography can be beneficial as you disciple your family. This also encourages our learning from those gifted to teach in the body of Christ. And remember, we are not relegated only to the teachers of today. By God's grace, many of the great teachers given to the church throughout its history can be read and interacted with. All we need to do is pick up one of these readily accessible books and start reading.

Chapter 5

Our Manner of Worship

_____

In the last chapter, we examined the *means* by which we are to worship God in our families. It is also important that we worship God in the right *manner* within our families. This involves being reverent, joyful, regular and consistent.

REVERENT

First and foremost, we must be reverent in worship. Unfortunately, when we think of "reverence," cold and stiff formalism often comes to mind. But this is not reverence. Reverent worship is nothing more than giving God due respect, honor, and adoration in light of who He is. This is fitting and right. This means that we need to be careful not to treat God casually. We are not here concerned with whether your family is in their pajamas or in suits and dresses. Rather, we are speaking about the attitude we set in our family worship. It is good to note that worship may be a lot of things, but it is never casual. Worship is an encounter with the living, true, holy, sovereign God of the universe. Just think about these encounters with God in Scripture that involve worship: Moses takes off his shoes (Exod. 3), Israel is fearful (Exod. 20), Isaiah quakes (Isa. 6), Job silences his lips (Job 40), John falls down as though dead (Rev. 1). Even the elders and angels, who are worshiping day in and day out before the throne, aren't casual in their worship (Isa. 6; Rev. 4). Casual worship of the living, true, holy, sovereign God of the universe just doesn't exist!

How should this look in our homes? Again, this doesn't mean that our worship time must be cold or stiff. Rather, as an example of desiring to have our worship in the home marked by reverence, we should seek to direct our conversation in family worship, so that it is not diverted to the chores that need to be done, the schedule for the upcoming week, or the television shows on later that night. Or, we may want to reinforce the need to listen to the Scripture reading with care or that when we are singing, it is to God that we are lifting our voices. On the other hand, the head of the home must make sure that he doesn't commit the error that is too often made of mistaking severity for reverence.

JOYFUL

Worship that is biblical is not only reverent but also joyful! In worship, we are hearing the promises of God, meeting with Him, singing songs of adoration and praise, confessing our belief in this glorious God, and offering prayers to Him. How could we ever truly worship without joy? When we understand the truths of the Bible and those truths resonate in our very soul, joy naturally follows. And when we have a high view of God, which leads us to reverence, there should be an eruption of joy when we are worshiping God. This cannot be contrived or created.

However, this fruit of the Christian life can be encouraged and sought. As we lead our families in worship, we will want to model joyfulness in the presence of the Lord. We want them to see our true delight in meeting with God and celebrating Christ our Lord. As Psalm 16 says, "You make known to me the path of life; in your presence there is fullness of joy; at your right hand are pleasures forevermore."

However, having said this, there are moments in our family worship that should be marked with solemnity and even grief. For instance, we may pray for confession of sin or sing a psalm of lament; however, there is joy in the end in knowing that our sin is forgiven in Christ and that He binds all our wounds.

REGULAR AND CONSISTENT

Ideally, our practice of family worship should be regular and consistent. We should aim and strive to worship with our families daily. But this is easier said than done, isn't it? This is probably the number one struggle for families in our day and age. A father just said to me this past week, "We have had good seasons and bad with family worship. It feels like we are up and down. This month we are pretty consistent, and the next two months not so much."

Anyone who has practiced family worship knows this struggle. However, it is good to continually remind ourselves that there is nothing that will dilute the benefits and effects of family worship more than family worship that is sporadically practiced. An athlete getting her body into shape does not work out sporadically. She will never be in top shape if that is the approach she takes. It is her consistent and devoted attendance to exercise over months that will produce the greatest fruit. It is the same with family worship.

There are also very real biblical theological reasons to practice family worship daily. The Lord taught us in the Lord's Prayer to pray for "our daily bread" (Matt. 6:11). We are told to "pray without ceasing" (1 Thess. 5:17). Fathers are told to teach their children "when [they] lie down, and when [they] rise" (Deut. 6:7). These are commands for individual Christians, but the principles of these passages and others (Job 1:5; Ps. 1:2; Dan. 6:10; Phil. 4:6; 1 Tim. 5:5; etc.) should translate to our family as well. It is difficult to pray for "our daily bread" and to "pray without ceasing" in our home if our family worship is not regular.

There are some who would advocate practicing family worship twice a day (my family is doing well to maintain once a day—and most weeks that is a struggle, but what a blessing if you can do it!). In the Old Testament, sacrifices were offered in the morning and evening. There is evidence to suggest that the New Testament church offered prayers in the morning and evening as well. It is also reasonable that we would begin our day with the family in worship, setting our minds upon Him and asking for God's blessing of the day, and closing the day with worship as a family and asking forgiveness for the sins committed and giving thanksgiving for the day's blessings. There is a great benefit to "bookending" the day with worship in our home. But for some families this will not work. The head of the home must be sensitive to the patterns of the life of his/her family and make a wise and pastoral decision about the frequency of family worship in the home. Heads of the home must remember that they are under-shepherds caring for the flock. Love and gentleness must be marks of their headship, so we must seek to be sensitive to what works for our families.

We also need to be consistent in our practice of family worship. We do not want to give mixed messages to our family members by approaching it lackadaisically one night and seriously the next. Our consistency in emphasis and approach will have lasting effect upon the seriousness with which our family attends to worship in the home. As we think about family worship, we should endeavor to approach God every day with resolve, focus, and "heart-felt" faith.

However, having said that family worship must be regular and consistent does not mean that it has to be perfect! We too often do injury to our families by seeking perfection in our practices or even our persons. Fathers, especially need to hear this: Your family worship will never be perfect! It doesn't have to be. And there are times that it won't be regular and consistent. Whenever you realize that your family worship hasn't been regular and consistent lately, remember that it is a means of grace, not a burden to bear, so just pick it back up and start again. It is good to remind ourselves that every family goes through different seasons. There may be times when my family is joyful, and other times that it seems like anything but joyful. We may have a couple of weeks in which our family's interaction with Scripture, praying of prayers, and singing of hymns seems to be marked by an uncommon reverence, and other weeks that it seems to be treated casually. Through all seasons, be patient, be gracious, and keep praying that God would bless. He isn't looking for perfection; that standard has been met by Christ. Rest and enjoy what you have, while all the while striving and praying that your family worship becomes even more reverent, joyful, regular and consistent.

CHAPTER 6

What Family Worship is Not

We have looked at what family worship is, and now we will articulate what it is not. Family worship can be abused and used to abuse. We must make sure that we do not allow our family to go down either one of these paths.

REPLACEMENT FOR CORPORATE WORSHIP

Family worship is not a replacement for corporate worship. There are some who have begun abandoning corporate worship for "Do-it-at-home church." As we pointed out earlier in the book, corporate worship is essential for our family's spiritual life. We may thoroughly enjoy our time of family worship at home and there may be much fruit born from it, but this cannot lead us away from the church gathered together. Family worship is not a replacement for corporate worship with the diverse and multi-gifted body of Christ. Rather, it is a different sphere. We do not skip the Sunday morning service for a time with the family around the kitchen table, no matter what we are doing around that table! In the language of a previous age, Richard Baxter made this same point by saying, "You must not be hearing the master of a family, when you should be in a church hearing the pastor."[1] The head of the home who is leading his/her family out of the corporate worship service to practice family worship at home is doing great damage to the spiritual lives of those under his/her care; no matter how much he/she thinks otherwise!

WORSHIP OF THE FAMILY

Years ago a pastor shared with me his concern about some families and their newfound love for family worship. There was a dear man in his congregation who loved the Lord and loved his family. He was incredibly gifted, and the church needed him to use his gifts in its midst. However, every time the pastor asked him to serve he replied that he could not. He could not serve any weeknight, because it would take him away from home and worshiping with his family. He could not serve any Sunday morning or evening, because he needed to sit with his family in church and Sunday School. He couldn't serve on Saturday, because that was an entire day devoted to his family and enjoying each other. His care and love for his family was admirable, but it led him to some misguided conclusions. What he didn't understand is that the church *and* his family were suffering from his loving his family too much!

There are undercurrents in the evangelical world right now that place too much emphasis upon the family. We can worship the family just as easily as we can worship wealth or Buddha. And they are equally idolatrous. As we practice family worship, we do not want our world to begin to revolve around our family. Another way of saying this is, we don't want to worship the

---

1   Baxter, Directory, p. 414.

family, we want worshiping families. There is a big difference. A family that is truly worshiping God together will naturally find itself looking outward and engaging more and more with people beyond their home. This is an appropriate response of our growth in grace. As we grow more in love with God we grow more in love with people. Those two things cannot be separated. They are two sides of the same coin. "Love the Lord your God with all your heart and with all your soul and with all your mind" and "love your neighbor as yourself" (Matt. 22:37, 39).

A BURDEN OR WEIGHT

This bears mentioning again: Family worship is an instrument through which God gives us grace...it is not something that should be a burden. It is a joy. Since it is not to be a burden, we should not be hard on ourselves if we miss a night. What often happens is that a family will miss a night, then two, then three, then a week, and never pick it back up again. Often this happens because it feels as if we are having to start a huge task all over again, and the burden is just too great. As I tell friends and remind myself—if you a miss a night, fine—pick it back up the next night. If you miss two nights or three nights or even a week—fine—do not beat yourself up—just pick it right back up. Family worship, like all kinds of worship, is a means of grace and is not to be viewed as a burden or a task to be accomplished. It is something we do in response to God's grace, not to earn it. We often approach it legalistically, and doing so not only kills the joy of worshiping God, but is antithetical to the relationship rooted in grace that we have with God. Worship is not to be a weight around our necks, but a means of lifting our heads up. Therefore, if it is a hard week, do not heap guilt upon your and your family's shoulders for missing family worship; just pick it right back up. This is no different than the struggles many of us find in maintaining secret worship. It is the same struggle with the same remedy: by God's grace we apply ourselves to it again.

Also, we must not expect too much, especially at the beginning. We should start slow. The family worship bulletin I have used at a couple of churches I have had the privilege to serve is simple. It is just a Scripture chapter to be read, a catechism question and answer to read, a Bible verse to memorize (if desired), a hymn to sing, and a prayer focus. A family could easily enjoy a night of family worship with all of these elements in fifteen minutes. But even that may be too much for some families. It is for us some nights. If that is true for you on any particular day, then just read the Scripture and pray a prayer. If a father is not comfortable explaining the Scripture, then just read it without explanation. Start slowly…but start. And don't make it a huge burden and weight around your family's neck.

A TIME TO CASTIGATE

Some will attempt to use family worship as an opportunity to castigate and rebuke other family members. In some houses, every Scripture read seems to be an opportunity for Dad to tell the children to behave and his wife to honor him. Family worship is not the time to press a personal agenda or to "call out" other family members and their sin. If there is offense in the home, then this should be addressed before the family enters into worship. It should not be a time that the children dread because "here Dad goes again." We would do well to remember Paul's admonition in Colossians 3:21, "Fathers, do not provoke your children, lest they become discouraged." Family worship should fix a family's eyes upon Christ above all else and not upon the sins of one another. However, there may be times that the family as a whole decides that they need to confess a family sin before God or need to address a pervasive issue in the family. And fathers should lead in this. Just make sure that this isn't "your" agenda and a nightly routine. A true servant leader will understand the difference.

CHRISTIAN FAMILY ACTIVITIES

We have discussed this in other chapters, so we will only address it briefly here. Family worship is not Christian family activity night. It is a blessing when families gather together to read a good Christian book, do a fun craft, or even do a night of Bible skits. However, this is not family worship. Family worship is centered on the elements God has given us to worship Him: specifically, the reading of the Bible, prayer, and song (and, in corporate worship, the sacraments). These are appointed by God for His worship and are the most beneficial for our families. These other activities could be added to our family worship or engaged in at other times during the week, but we should be careful that they do not take the place of family worship.

MORALITY TRAINING

Many Christians would quickly leave a church in which the sermon each week was just a lesson on morality (unfortunately, many wouldn't!). Most Christians understand that we are not moralists. This does not mean that we don't believe in morals. We do, but we don't believe in morals for morality's sake. A Christian wants to see individuals living moral lives as fruit of the inward change that has been wrought by God's grace poured out upon their hearts. Ironically, some of us who would quickly leave a church that was teaching simple morality will do this very thing with our children at home. We fall into the trap of turning family worship into the zenith of morality training. This is not the proper goal or purpose of family worship. Family worship is, first and foremost, *worship*. We are not aiming to just produce little moralists running around knowing right from wrong. We want to see our children's lives changed according to the gospel, and we want them to live their lives in light of that change. That should be every Christian parent's desire. And how does that change happen? By God working through His Word.

A Guarantee

Most Christian parents desire above all else that their children come to saving faith in Christ. I have sat with many weeping parents concerned for the souls of their grown children. And there is this tendency within us to try to find some magical procedure or strategy by which we can guarantee the salvation of our children and avoid the pain we have witnessed in older parents. Dear friends, there is no such thing. There are Isaacs and Ishmaels. We can teach, we can share the "Good News," we can hope, we can labor, and we can pray. And we are to do those things with all the energy and determination that God has given to us, but then we are to leave our children in the Lord's hands. I say all of this to underscore the fact that practicing family worship is not a guarantee that our children will come to saving faith. It is a tool which He may use. It is a helpful means for our children to hear the gospel of grace and see faith modeled before them, but it is no magical pill. If you happen to be one of those parents whose children have grown, left the home, and still have not yielded their lives to Christ, I grieve with you. But it is not an empty grief. We have hope that the seeds which you have planted through the years will bear fruit in due season. You have shared the testimony of Christ with your children. You have pointed them to Him by your words and life, not perfectly, but you have pointed them. Who among us would say they have done it well, let alone perfectly? Regardless of our family's present circumstances, we can continue to pray, trust, and hope that the Lord will use the years of scattered seed and call our prodigal children to Himself. He is worthy of our trust and hope.

Family worship is a true blessing, but for it to be so, as we have discussed in this chapter, we need to safeguard what it is and also not force foreign expectations upon it. As you begin to practice family worship in your home, it will become apparent that the Lord in all His wisdom appointed this practice for the benefit of His people. At times it may seem odd and awkward, and it may be tempting to do other things in its place. But in the end, you will look back and thank God for every evening that was spent with your family in worship—you won't regret one.

CHAPTER 7

Helps for the Journey

Today, there are very few individuals in the Western church who grew up worshiping in their homes, so most of us are starting from a limited knowledge base and with very little to absolutely no experience in family worship. Therefore, let's look at a few practical helps that may aid our families in this new journey.

FIND THE BEST TIME

This involves trial and error, but most families function at some times of the day better than other times of the day. Some children (and parents!) do not do well in the early morning hours before they have had their cup of coffee. Yes, I know of a family where the kids drink a cup of coffee in the morning, and the parents would tell you that it is needed! If that is the case, don't try to do family worship at that time. Some mothers and fathers come home exhausted from work and need some time to rest before engaging with everyone, so maybe this is not the optimum time for these families to worship. Other families function best in the morning and may choose to do family worship immediately following breakfast or before the children leave for school. A young married couple may choose to worship during the lunch hour when the husband or wife comes home. For some families it works best to worship after dinner or before bed. Try different times of the day and see what works best for everyone. Every family is different. We all have our own rhythms. Just find the right rhythm for your family.

SAME TIME

My wife teases me sometimes when she sees a schedule that I have laid out for myself. I have different activities appointed at different times. I will have my private worship penciled in for 6 am to 6:45 am, a meeting with a member of the church scheduled from 9am to 10:30am, and then she will see that I have "family time" penciled in for 5pm to 8pm. When she is feeling a little ornery she will say, "You have to schedule your family?" She is joking, but if she were serious I would have to reply, "Yes." Otherwise, other things begin to encroach upon this time which is important for the health of our family. I don't want my children or wife being neglected. And it is too easy for the phone call I answered at 4:45 pm to run until 5:30 pm I need to be able to say to the person on the other end of the line, and to myself, that I must go, because I have promised that 5 pm to 8 pm is our time together. There are many good things that can and will fill our schedules. Therefore, if we don't pencil in the things which matter the most, they often get neglected and suffer at the expense of other good things in life. Just like other important tasks, family worship must be scheduled. For each family this will be different. Regardless of when you pencil in the time, make it an appointed time. That does not mean that family worship has to occur at 6 pm every night. The appointed time may be a "semi-fixed" time. There are some nights that dinner isn't over by 6 pm. Don't be rigid, but do have a consistent and routine time that your family knows they will be gathering for worship. Otherwise it will seldom happen. Other things will get in the way.

SAME PLACE

As important as having the same time for family worship is, it is also helpful to have it in the same place. Some families gather around the kitchen or dining room table. I have had the pleasure of being at dinner with multiple families who open their Bibles immediately before or after the meal while everyone is seated around the table. Others may choose to sit in the living room or on the back porch. It doesn't really matter where it is, it just helps if the "where" is consistent in your home. This is especially helpful for young children. My son and daughter know that when we say it is time for family worship, we are all off to the family room. When my daughter was younger, she used to barely be able to climb up on the couch, but right up on the couch she would go when it was time for family worship. She would snuggle right in between her mother and father. She knew that she was supposed to sit still on the couch during our time of family worship and wasn't to get up until we had our closing prayer. This was a relief to her parents. We didn't have to wrestle with her every week and teach her once again that she must sit still in this new place or that. Children thrive in the known and regular. Consistency in the place you have family worship will help them to settle their minds and rein in those child energies. Meeting in the same place also minimizes distractions. It is familiar and common ground for family worship, and so eyes are less tempted to be distracted.

Start Slow

We are beginning the process of returning the church to this important discipline. Hopefully, our children will be able to take it a step farther, but for most of us this is a very new practice. Therefore, do not expect too much too early or even expect too much from your family in the long run. Many heads of homes will be convicted about the need for family worship and begin to lead their families in it. However, zeal may lead them (especially fathers!) to try to get their family to run before they are even crawling. Fathers, don't ask your children to start memorizing Leviticus in the first few weeks of family worship! Just start by reading a small portion of Scripture, praying a short prayer, and singing a song. As *everyone* in the family grows in worshiping together, there will be the ability and desire to make it fuller.

Brevity

Family worship should not be a burden, but many times we turn it into a burden by making it too long. Young families especially need to keep this in mind because of their young children. Those just beginning family worship would also be well advised to keep it short. It is amazing how much quality worship can take place in fifteen or even ten minutes. Some families may find that fifteen minutes is too short for their family. Great! But not all or even most families should aim at having a half-hour of worship each evening. I know it doesn't work for our family at this point. Over time this may change as your family matures in age and/or faith. However, the length of time our family engages in worship is not a commentary on our family's maturity in the faith. Remember what Jesus said about the scribes and their long prayers (Mark 12:40; Luke 20:47): They were a pretense and for show. Longer doesn't always mean better.

MAKE IT A PRIORITY

If family worship is going to succeed in the long run, it must be a high priority in the home. This means that we need to be careful that other things don't take its place in our schedules. A family which is seldom home together is a family that cannot worship together. Reading the Bible on the way to gymnastics or soccer practice might be a great idea, but it's not the same as regular family worship at home. We must make our worship together as a family a priority. Does this mean family members can't have other things on their schedule? Absolutely not! However, it does mean that our schedules can't be jam-packed. The modern-day Western Christian needs to hear this. In addition, it is not always community activities or children's sports that fill our schedules; often, it is the church. It is important that we serve in the church and enter into dynamic fellowship with our brothers and sisters in Christ. However, if my family and I are engaged in church activities four nights a week, then we aren't home together consistently. We may be doing good things. Our family and others may benefit, but we can't be so involved in the activities of the church that we neglect the ministry we are called to in our family. Busyness (even with church activities) does not equal godliness.

BE FLEXIBLE

Having made the last point and the point above about the importance of establishing a time for family worship, I also want to underscore the importance of being flexible in our approach to family worship. First, there will be days that it just doesn't work. If this is a regular occurrence, then we may need to adjust when or where we are having family worship. However, some days it just won't work at all, no matter what provisions we have put in place, and our family has to wait until tomorrow, the next day, or even the day after that. That is fine! Family worship is an instrument or means of grace, not a burden that our family is to struggle under. Second, be flexible in approach. Some nights our family is just tired, and the normal twenty minutes of worship may be too much. We may just choose to read a short psalm, pray the Lord's Prayer together, and sing "Jesus Loves Me." Having flexibility in our approach will save us a lot of heartache and our families a great deal of stress. As we think about worship, it is good to remind ourselves that God has given us abounding grace in Christ Jesus. In fact, it is by that very grace that we are able to worship Him. It is grace welling up in our hearts that moves us with desire to offer Him praise from those thankful hearts. If that is the case, and it is, then let's extend ourselves and the members of our family a touch of that grace in the way we approach family worship. How good it is to not only know *of* the grace of Christ, but to know and live *in* the grace of Christ!

MODEL THE RIGHT ATTITUDE

Our attitudes have a lot to do with our experiences. And others are always watching our attitudes. Husbands will want to model the right attitude before their wives and parents will want to model the right attitude before their children. Children are incredibly intuitive. I don't have to tell my children that candle and sewing stores are not my favorite destinations. In the same way, they know when Mom and Dad are just going through the motions or are begrudgingly calling the family together in worship. It is quite another thing altogether when Mom and Dad talk about looking forward to worship and exercise a consistent joy in the midst of family worship. As one old writer said,

"Gloominess, or austerity of devotion, will make them think it is a hard service. Let them be met with smiles. Let them be met as friends. Let them be met as for the most delightful service in which they can be engaged."[1] Over time, these attitudes will affect the climate of your home and everyone's approach not only to worship, but to life.

PERSEVERANCE

Maybe the most important advice for family worship is to persevere in it. There will be moments and even weeks where it seems like a chore and that little fruit is being born. Your toddler has trouble sitting still or maybe even your teenager! Your oldest child complains every night or the tune keeps getting lost in the middle of singing. Regardless of the discouragements that are thrown your way, just keep going! You are not alone, and your situation is not unique! Some nights family worship in our home resembles a comedy show more than it does a gathering before the throne of God! A couple of years ago, we were reading from a section of Proverbs. Of course in Proverbs there is a constant refrain regarding the way of the righteous versus the way of the wicked. And I was explaining what wicked meant. My daughter, who was five at the time, first thought I was saying "winking," and so she kept winking her eyes. Once we got past that, she thought I was saying "wiggling." And so we had that acted out. Finally, she said, "Oh, so wicked like the dogs in Bambi II." Well, they are mean and vicious, so I thought to myself, "This is an alright illustration," so I made the mistake of saying, "Yes, they are wicked." Of course, my son, who was going through

---

1   James Waddell Alexander, *Thoughts on Family Worship* (Philadelphia, PA: Presbyterian Board of Publication, 1847. Reprinted by BiblioBazaar, LLC), p. 195.

a phase where he repeated things he liked, began repeating the words "Dogs" and "Bambi" over and over. Our family worship derailed at that point. I couldn't get the two of them to stop thinking and talking about Bambi. Every time we took it back to Proverbs, somehow Bambi and those wicked dogs reentered the conversation. My advice for times like these is, pick it back up the next night. Keep enduring and persevering in gathering with your family in worship. Perseverance is the best remedy for all these ills. Over time, most of them will be overcome and fruit which was invisible at the time will begin to show itself in the future.

CHAPTER 8

But, What if ...

My hope is that most of us will be convicted of the importance and blessing of family worship. However, a conviction does not always result in action. As sinners, we are quick to excuse ourselves and rationalize to a point that we can deny our convictions without too much guilt. Others may choose to start family worship in their homes, but for some of us, discouragement sets in and convictions are tossed to the side of the road after months of struggling. This chapter will not address every possible scenario, but here are a few of the common struggles that often present themselves when we think of family worship and our own family.

Single Parents

I was raised for most of my life with a single mother and have seen up close the daily struggle of parenting alone. There are few single working mothers or fathers who come home with a lot of extra energy. And then they must still cook dinner, clean the dishes, inquire about their children's days, help with homework, prepare the children for bed, prepare tomorrow's lunches—the list goes on and on. It can make for a tiring and long day. The single mother or father has in reality taken on the responsibilities of both parents. This is far from easy. Single parents are to be honored and commended for their tireless labor. However, we still want to encourage single parents to lead their children in worship. It is not clear whether Timothy in the Scriptures had a father at home, but it is clear that his grandmother, Lois, and his mother, Eunice, took up the charge of raising Timothy in the gospel. It is their faith that they passed on to him as a good deposit. And Paul calls it to Timothy's remembrance (2 Tim. 1). What a legacy Lois and Eunice left! Dear single parent, it would also be the greatest gift you can give to your children, and family worship is one of the greatest tools we have for passing on our treasured faith.

I Feel Inadequate

This is usually one of the greatest barriers to the starting of family worship in our homes. This comes in two different forms. The first is that the head of the house feels inadequate to lead his/her family in worship because he/she is quite aware of the fact that he/she is a sinner. And furthermore, the rest of the family knows it! But the fact that he/she is a sinner and knows it is itself a qualification to lead his family in worship. It is the heart that has been turned from a heart of stone to a heart of flesh that is responsive to the Law of God. It is the regenerate believer who is pricked in conscience and grieves over his sin. It is also the regenerate believer who knows the mercy and grace found only in Christ Jesus. It is to Him that the head of the home is pointing his/her family; this Lord who he/she is able to call Savior. Our sin does not disqualify us from service in the

Lord's Kingdom. If that were the case, no pastor could stand before a congregation on any Sunday morning. And no father, husband, or mother could lead their family in worship. We are all sinners who are recipients of God's grace. In this life, those who have come to know Christ are sinner and saint at the same time. A Christian father, husband, or mother will be both, and this is no disqualification, but his/her very qualification.

Second, there are many who feel inadequate to lead their family in worship because they are not comfortable praying before their family or teaching from the Bible. We cannot allow this trepidation to deter us from doing that which is essential. A father, husband, or mother who feels this way should begin simply. For example, instead of not praying due to anxiety over publically praying, you could try opening the Bible to Matthew 6 and praying through the Lord's Prayer. However, we must not rest here, but out of love for Christ we want to seek to grow in our prayer life. As you begin pouring out your heart (Ps. 62:6) before God in secret worship your prayers will grow in maturity. You will become more comfortable in prayer, and this will eventually translate into praying with and for your family.

Our inadequate knowledge of the Scriptures and fear of teaching our spouse or children should also not stop us from practicing family worship. Start slow and trust God. If you aren't comfortable teaching or making a comment upon the Scriptures which have been read, then don't. As time passes and you grow in your faith and Bible knowledge, it will become second nature to ask questions and point out the central theme of the Bible reading that night. Douglas Kelly has some insightful and pastoral words for us on this subject:

> Remember this significant fact: a few direct, simple, and heartfelt words from one's own parent make far more impression on any

child than the most eloquent flow of fine instruction from an outsider. Our real problem as parents is not our lack of ability in praying, reading, or commenting, but is rather our underestimation of the immense power and influence God has given us to shape our offspring for His glory simply by virtue of the representative covenant relationship that is ours as parents who are "in Christ."[1]

UNBELIEVING SPOUSE

This is one of the more difficult scenarios to deal with, and our approach should differ a little bit depending on whether the husband or wife is the Christian. Christian wives will always want to honor their husbands (Eph. 5:22). Some of the most faithful Christians in the world are wives living with unbelieving husbands, and their love for Christ is manifested in the way that they continually honor their husbands. This must be the guiding principle in the Christian wife's actions here as in every part of her married life. The Christian wife living with an unbelieving husband will want to understand and value this first. Then she can move on to how she approaches family worship in her home. There is that wonderful question of Paul's in 1 Corinthians 7 where he says to a Christian woman married to an unbelieving husband, "Wife, how do you know whether you will save your husband?" The example of the wife's faith and character is often used by the Lord in drawing the unbelieving husband to Himself. It is difficult for a Christian wife to testify faithfully about the goodness of her Lord if she is undermining and disrespecting her husband. Therefore, above all else she will want to be careful to respect him in her approach, for he is making an assessment of Christ based upon her actions.

---

1   Kelly, p. 121.

Dear Christian sister in this circumstance, I would encourage you to approach your husband in all gentleness and wisdom and ask if he might consider joining you in reading the Bible daily. Most likely, he will not join with you in singing, but he may join with you in reading the Bible and join with you praying a short prayer (if you pray it). If he is unwilling, then you may let him know that you will be on the couch each evening at such-and-such a time to read the Bible and pray and that you would be delighted if he would join you sometime. Now you must consistently be there. If he does not join you, in your time of prayer always pray that the Lord would move your husband to join you tomorrow night. It may be that you will be a living example to him of worship for years before he responds, but it will be hard for him not to witness your nightly worship of the Lord in your home. It may be that on some evening he will begin to join you. There are two things to be cautious about when taking this approach: First, be careful that your worship does not turn into a show for your husband. You are providing a witness, and yet your worship must still be focused upon God. Second, be careful not to exasperate your husband by pressuring him too much to join you. Continue to pray and in the right moments with wisdom remind him that he is welcome to join you, which would delight your soul. Who knows, dear sister, you just might "save your husband."

Christian husbands will always want to love their wives well. This should be the controlling influence for the Christian husband in his marriage relationship and therefore also in his approach to family worship in the home with an unbelieving wife. I would encourage the Christian husband to approach his wife with love and inform her that because he loves her he would like to read the Scriptures and pray together nightly. He must make sure that she knows that it will be a safe place and not a time in which he is going to "brow-beat" her. He may even tell her that he would like her to pick the Scripture to read each evening. If she is unwilling, then he should take the same approach as that offered to the wife of an unbelieving husband above. He should inform her that he will be on the couch each evening at such and such a time and that he would desire nothing more than her joining him. Each evening she should see him there. He also must make sure that he does not turn family worship into a show for his wife. He must be careful that he does not act in an unloving way towards her.

If there are children in the home then the believing spouse should try to have family worship with the children even if the unbelieving spouse is unwilling to participate. It will be difficult to reinforce the importance of worship in the home with your children if their father or mother refuses to engage, but this does not mean that it is impossible. Your frustration will reach high points and you will want to "throw in the towel," but don't. Persevere and continue to encourage your children in worship. Family worship should be a positive experience, and your joy in approaching family worship will greatly influence your children; by God's grace, your spouse will be influenced as well.

CHRISTIAN SPOUSE, BUT NOT ON BOARD

There are some of us that will find ourselves married to Christians who do not see the need or benefit of family worship. Sometimes they are just concerned and fearful of the unknown or what is required of them if they willingly join in. The best course of action here is patience. Be patient, respectful, and loving toward your spouse. Pray that the Lord would give them the same conviction that you have. Find out why they have reservations and seek to understand the reasoning behind these. Again, I would encourage the convicted spouse to appoint a time, invite their mate, and start worshiping daily at that hour. If you are winsome in your approach to your Christian spouse and faithful in your pursuit, the Lord often blesses and our spouses begin to willingly join us. Be gentle and start slow when they do join you. Let me say by way of encouragement that I have seen many Christian families where one spouse was opposed to starting family worship now enjoying family worship as an entire family.

CHILDREN OF DIFFERENT AGES

Having children of different ages is a blessing during family worship. However, many struggle with the different abilities of their children and how to approach family worship because of it. One of the first times I witnessed family worship was in a family with six children. I immediately noticed the way that the various ages were brought together in this nightly event. It was a delight to watch the older children help the younger children. They were turning the Bible pages and showing them the passage with their fingers. The older children seemed to take pride in this responsibility. The younger children seemed to enjoy having the special attention of their older brothers and sisters. If the older children are memorizing the catechism or memory verses that are too difficult for the younger children, it is helpful to give the younger children special responsibilities in each family worship gathering. They may lead the family in singing the doxology or offer the closing prayer. For the youngest, they may just be charged with getting the Bibles and hymnals and passing them out to the other family members. Even a two-and-a-half-year-old is able to do this and enjoy it. Use the different age levels for the benefit of everyone. Our youngest loves to tell the rest of us the order of prayer, "Daddy first, sister second, Mommy third, and I will pray last."

CHILDREN SITTING STILL

In the beginning and when we have children of young ages, we will often find ourselves wrestling with our children to sit still more than we are worshiping (as a father of a four-year-old little boy, some nights I feel more like a cross between a piñata and a gymnast than a worshiper). But this wrestling is a necessary "evil." If you put in the time, it will pay dividends down the road. With young children, have them initially sit on Mom or Dad's lap. When they master sitting still, then have them move to a place on the couch or floor between Mom and Dad. Eventually they will learn to sit still, but you must be consistent and determined. And this will wonderfully translate to corporate worship as well.

LACK OF RESPONSE

At times, you may face a situation like this: It has been weeks of frustration and complaining from the children about another night of family worship. You couldn't believe that it was possible, but the singing has actually become worse, and eyes seem to glaze over as the Scriptures are read. There is no response and you are tired. Leading family worship feels like work. We have all been there. Don't stop! Who knows what seeds are being planted and what work the Lord is doing beneath the surface! The world measures success by what they see, but as Christians, we know that our eyes often deceive us. Fight discouragement and keep going. We will spend years and countless hours of frustration working on our golf swing or learning to cook; we should have even more determination to follow through on family worship. But we can have more than determination; we have firmly rooted hope. God has promised to work by His Word—rely upon it! Do not give up! Trust the Lord and persevere.

LUKEWARMNESS

This is not a barrier that most of us would recognize, but one of the greatest struggles, not only in maintaining family worship, but in the Christian life, is our lukewarm faith. When we really boil it down, we just don't want our lives to center around Christ and worshiping Him. It is easy to confess that we want this, but in reality, other things are more important to us and our family. We take time daily to keep the home clean, rest by watching television, and attend our children's activities, but finding time to worship each day seems too involved. Lukewarmness has a hold of our hearts (Rev. 3:15-16).

I think we all know this trap and how easy it is to fall into. And so we resolve to fight it and to seek Christ. The problem is often this is still lukewarm, because we are seeking Him by our own strength. White hot, affection-moved, mind-engaged, heart-transformed, love-compelled, soul-enlivened pursuit of Christ will only be found as we abide in Him and He in us (John 15). It is to Him that we must run. Do so in prayer and ask that according to the riches of His glory He may grant you to be strengthened with power through His Spirit in your inner be-ing, so that Christ may dwell in your heart through faith—that you, being rooted and grounded in love may have strength to comprehend with all the saints what is the breadth and length and height and depth, and to know the love of Christ that sur-passes knowledge, that you may be filled with the fullness of God (Eph. 3:14-19). His grace is sufficient and effective. If it can take stone hearts and turn them to flesh (Ezek. 36:26), His grace is sufficient to turn lukewarm hearts into furnaces burning hot for His glory. Do you doubt it? Then remember how Paul closes this prayer in Ephesians: And we know that He is "able to do far more abundantly than all that we ask or think, according to the power at work within us" (Eph. 3:20). It is to this God that we offer our worship. "To him be glory in the church and in Christ Jesus throughout all generations, forever and ever. Amen" (Eph. 3:21). How worthy of our worship He is in our lives, our churches, and our homes.

CHAPTER 9

Just Do It

Nike has made a lot of money with their advertising slogan, "Just Do It." We can talk about family worship, its importance, its impact, and how to practice it, but we are not getting anywhere unless we just do it! Our families have been starved for a couple of generations now. We have allowed the center of the Christian family to drift, and the church has suffered. Isn't it time that the evangelical church begins worshiping in the home again? Family worship is time tested and God appointed. Let's not wait any longer to begin.

It is my constant prayer and hope that the Lord will lead the evangelical church through a time of revival. Then that this revival within the church would spread into an awakening throughout the world. But we cannot speak about the Christian faith impacting our world, our country, or our community if it is not first impacting our homes—and few things will bring our Christian faith to bear in the home more than family worship. We cannot cry out for the need for evangelism and others coming to faith, so that there are more worshipers before the throne, if we are not committed to worship ourselves—and this includes worship in the home. We cannot complain about our children wandering from the faith if we are not making it the center of their upbringing in our home—and though family worship may not be the only way, it is surely one of the most beneficial ways. In light of this, it is time that we return to the Christian practice of family worship. Let it begin with my home and your home. And by God's grace it will spread to homes within our churches and in homes throughout the land. But someone must begin... and why not you and your family? As Matthew Henry said, "Be persuaded brethren, thus to dedicate your houses to God, and beg him to come and take possession of them. If you never did it, do it tonight with all possible seriousness and sincerity."[1] Amen. Just do it!

It is always helpful to hear testimonies of God's work in the lives of others. I always find it to be an encouragement to hear what God is doing, and I am sure that you do as well. Therefore, we are closing this book with a few testimonies from families that have experienced the revival of family worship in their homes. None of them would confess to loving Christ as much as they want. Not a single individual in these testimonials believes they are living perfectly. Rather, they are all relying upon the grace of God found in Christ Jesus and seeking to pursue that grace in their homes. They know the struggles of the Christian life and the Christian family all too well and they have found family worship to be a great encouragement to their love for Christ and their living in Him.

---

1   Matthew Henry, *Family Religion: Principles for Raising a Godly Family* (Fearn, Ross-shire: Christian Heritage imprint of Christian Focus Publications, 2008), p. 32.

Carissa Minnaar, Young Wife and Mother

(MASON, MICHIGAN)

It's 8:15 on a Tuesday evening. The dinner dishes are almost done, the kids are in the basement running off their last bits of energy before bedtime, and my husband and I are trying to debrief from the day for a few minutes despite the deafening noise seeping up through the floorboards. The cry from someone below after running into a pole is our signal that it's time to call it a day...

"FAMILY WORSHIP!!" my husband yells down the stairs, and the kids run up and gather in the living room. For a long time we attempted to do family worship immediately after dinner when we were still gathered at the table, but the "Martha" in me was too often tempted to work in the kitchen while the kids were occupied listening to Dad, and soccer sometimes got in the way. Besides, half the kids would finish dinner in 2.5 minutes and be way too squirrelly by the time the rest of us were done, and we found ourselves failing more often than not. So now we gather together right before the younger kids go to bed to read, sing, and pray together. If the evening events are running late and we are tempted to skip it, one of the kids usually reminds us that we need to do family worship (even if it is sometimes used as a stalling technique and even if it sometimes feels like it should be called "family discipline time" rather than family worship time).

We have chosen a variety of options for the reading portion—from straight scripture to devotionals to story Bibles. My husband knows the current issues and needs of the family, and we have found that if a devotional is too prescriptive, it may not allow him to shepherd us as personally. So, we usually either read scripture directly or something like *The Gospel Story Bible,* which the kids enjoy; it leaves the questions up to us. The kids all love the singing time, although sometimes there are minor disputes about who gets to pick the song! The most frequent request is definitely "Holy, Holy, Holy" (or "Ho-wee, Ho-wee, Ho-wee," as our two-year-old sings it).

My favorite tradition that we have started in recent months is that we all kneel around the coffee table together when it is time to pray. We have one child who tends to daydream audibly, one child who wiggles so much she is often literally upside down on the couch by prayer time, and one child who might wander off while the rest of our eyes are closed. So, kneeling together has helped us all focus our attention on the task at hand. We want our kids to tangibly see that we are a family humbly submitting to the triune God at the close of every day. On a good night, after prayer time ends, the kids calmly walk upstairs arm in arm, with the hymns we've just sung echoing through their minds. Of course, it never quite looks like that. But our prayer is that even on one of the rougher nights, they are learning that the covenant-keeping God of our family knows them, loves them, and will go with them no matter how far they travel outside the walls of our home.

Ryan Kelly, Young Husband and Father

(CHESTER SPRINGS, PENNSYLVANIA)

I was a graduate student early in my marriage. Because my school schedule was radically different each day, and because even that changed every semester, my wife and I found it difficult to maintain a consistent time for family worship. This schedule instability then bred inconsistent worship. We'd have a few good days and then a drought. We'd start up again, but would have a good week followed by another drought. We became frustrated that every "restart" of our family worship seemed harder because of guilt over past failures. Our pastor reassured us, however, that it was never a failure to run back to God. Part of our sanctification is the Holy Spirit working through our weakness to produce more faithful devotion to our Lord. This encouragement has stayed with us, and even though droughts still come, we are reminded that our gracious God embraces us every time we turn back to him.

John Fernsler, Husband and Father

(BOSTON, MASSACHUSETTS)

"*Did God lie?*" That was the question that my oldest daughter, Meagan, asked after we read Genesis 9 during one of our family worship times. The chapter ends with "All the days of Noah were 950 years. And then he died." A bit surprised by the question, I inquired further… "What!?" She replied that a few chapters earlier that God had said that He was not going to allow man to live longer than 120 years (Gen. 6:3), so *did God lie?* We looked back and, sure enough, that is what it says. We had just recently started family worship times in our home, and I was surprised to learn that my kids were even paying attention—it did not seem like it anyway! For sure, they interacted during our times together—singing the hymns, taking turns praying, reciting the memory verses—but, I often wondered if they were getting anything out of the reading of the Scriptures and my brief commentaries on the passages. That all changed with one short, direct, and poignant question about the character of God. It was the first of many "serious" theological questions that my kids have asked me since which have not been limited to these times of worship but have spilled over into other talks as well.

I've noticed that when we gather for family worship, not only do we come together as a family, but the animals join us as well! The dogs normally lie down at the feet of the children, who are sitting on the couch, and the cats either sit in our kids' laps or on the furniture nearby. One time, our newest cat, Miki, had come to join us for worship and sat on the mantle above the fireplace. He sat there fairly motionless...until we started singing our hymn. Then he perked up and started looking at us directly, twisting his head and ears back and forth—like one hearing a song sung poorly! We started laughing so hard that we could barely finish the hymn. It was a new application to the admonition to "make a *joyful noise* to the Lord" (Ps. 100).

The singing of hymns together has brought us together in a way I did not expect. We are a family that likes music, but the gift to sing songs well was given to others. Through our off tune/off pitch voices, the Lord has brought about a deeper intimacy and unity between us, especially as we worship the Lord through music. My kids are also much more confident than they used to be when singing in church. Sometimes in our family worship we will read through a hymn and discuss the meaning of the words and phrases that we are singing. As a side benefit to all of this, all three of my children have desired to take music lessons with the anticipation of using their skills during our worship times together.

Prayer has also had a big impact on us as we worship together as a family. We are not only praying more frequently together before the Lord; it has also been very humbling to see how God is maturing my kids through prayer. Maggie, our youngest, for example, used to pray for everyone like this: "I pray that Grandpa and Grandma have a good time." Then, she started praying a little more specifically, "I pray that Grandpa and Grandma will be saved and that they will have a good time." Now, she is beginning to make requests like this:"I pray that Grandpa and Grandma will go to church this weekend and that you will save them so that they can be in heaven." I know that part of her prayer growth is just the fact that she is getting older, but the Lord has definitely developed within her a better understanding of the benefits of the saved and the needs of the lost, particularly her Grandparents. We used to keep a prayer journal during our family worship time, but that became very time consuming for us. We now focus on the daily and weekly events around us and in the world, highlighting God's answers to our prayers as we go along. When we focus our attention on the present and near future, our children see that God really works in the daily lives of His followers, and that has motivated them to pray even more.

Chad Bailey, Husband and Father
(STOCKBRIDGE, GEORGIA)

Family worship was a foreign concept to me until my college days in Jackson, MS, where, as a member at Trinity Presbyterian Church (PCA), I was introduced to it by one of the pastors. I look back on that time now and give many thanks to God for both that pastor, whom I still love, and for the desire that was born in me to lead my future family in worship in our home.

Before I was married, I picked up a copy of *The Family Worship Book* (Terry Johnson) from the church, and when we were wed, my wife and I began reading Scripture and praying together. As children came along, I implemented the teaching of the book more and more. Since the beginning there have always been challenges, but I tried to have my act together so that as children came along, it would be easy for them to just join in. Looking back, it is easy to spot my naïveté and ignorance. I had great visions of the perfect family gathered together on the couch delighting in the Lord. My expectations of having a "Puritan-like" home (I love the Puritans but had an unfair view of them) were quickly met with the challenges that come along with having children. The children weren't the main problem, of course! I was and am still the chief sinner leading fellow sinners.

Our path of gathering as a family daily for worship has not been easy or neat or always joyful and perfectly consistent. At times, there have been discipline issues with children, and at other times, there are interruptions by neighbors or the phone. Unless there is an emergency, we usually don't answer the phone or let anything intrude on our time together in worship, but that has been a mindset that has developed over the years. Though it isn't true every time, our children, by the tender mercies of God, actually look forward to family worship. It has been and continues to be a joy for our household. Our family has greatly benefited from many pastors over the years in learning what family worship is all about and how to do it. I've probably learned the theology of family worship best from Joel Beeke and Terry Johnson, but practically I've learned the most from faithful pastor Scott Pierce as I've watched him over the years lead his family in worship. I've come to realize that as a husband and father who is the chief of sinners, if God does not build it and watch over it, then worship in the Bailey home will surely be in vain. By the grace of God, I and my household will serve the Lord!

Paul Ingram, Husband and Empty Nester
(GRAND RAPIDS, MICHIGAN)

I remember my childhood family devotion. "Devotion" is in the singular since Dad only tried it once while I was around. The

Pauline passage he read referred prominently to "circumcision," a word I recall finding intriguing. This could explain why there was never a second attempt. My wife had one fewer childhood devotional experience than I did. No wonder Sheila and I came to marriage and parenthood a tad uncertain about the whether, how, and why of worship in the family circle! It sounded like something we ought to do, but we lacked a covenantal base to our thinking. After we understood Scripture better, we still struggled through a succession of approaches and programs in fits and starts. Now that our children are adults, I'm pleasantly shocked at how much they remember about our times of prayer and Scripture reading. It wasn't that Sheila and I were much good at bringing our family together before God. It was the merciful faithfulness of a God who delights to bless His covenant. It is our testimony that even pitifully feeble stumblings are used richly. We've never become adept at family worship. We still struggle as empty nesters. But we have been blessed beyond measure for every step in this agency of sanctifying grace.

Luke Jones, College Student

(LEXINGTON, NORTH CAROLINA)

Family worship is something that has had a huge impact on me. Our family started to practice it in an organized way when my parents began to homeschool us. Each day, my mom would gather my sisters and I and we would read through a chapter or two in the Bible and discuss it, or we would go through a Bible study book together. At times, it seemed like just something to take up time, but I am really glad that we did it because I have a very good knowledge of Scripture now. This form of our family worship was used until I was in middle school. It was about that time that we started having our family worship time after dinner. We also switched from my mother leading just the kids, to my dad leading the whole family in studying God's Word. It was pretty simple; we would just read a couple chapters in the Word and then my dad would ask us questions to see if we understood what the passage was saying. Then he would explain anything that was confusing us. I am very thankful that my parents did this with us because I have a much more advanced understanding of Scripture than I would have, had we not practiced family worship.

I am now engaged, and my fiancée and I try to read the Bible together whenever we can. Once we are married and starting a family, I have every intention of instituting family worship in my home. It is a great tool to point children to Christ and to help them have a good understanding of the Bible. It also serves to bring families close together on a level that no other activity can.

Leah Helopoulos, Mother of Young Children and Jason's wonderful wife

(HOLT, MICHIGAN)

"Lord, I pray that you will give me a new heart and help me to obey you. Thank you for dying on the cross, Jesus. I love you. I want to be in heaven with you," prayed my seven-year-old daughter during family worship. Such precious words! As a mom, hearing my children seek after the Lord warms my soul, because it is a blessing to see my children seek righteousness and truth. I feel like a lot of family worship is teaching our children the stories of the Bible (Deut. 6), presenting the gospel to them, and applying the Bible to life—or at least that is the shape that most of our family worship evenings take! We don't sit down and have a three hour Bible lesson, but these short, age-appropriate Bible readings have a great effect upon our children as they learn the overarching themes of Scripture. It has been fun to see their growing desire to read the Word themselves.

Family worship in our home has the added benefit of encouraging my own relationship with the Lord. Hearing the Word and praying together as a family has been a consistent and growing blessing.

I have also been encouraged by the way that family worship helps us keep short accounts with one another. If there is conflict between us, it makes it difficult to sing, "Holy, Holy, Holy", without first reconciling, seeking forgiveness and restoration from one another. Consistently coming before His throne and hearing the Word provides continual opportunity for hearts to change, minds to grow, affections to flourish, and relationships to deepen.

Some nights are harder than others as the dog is jumping on the couch and the room seems chaotic, but I have seen how small, consistent times of worship in our home have provided long-term benefits. It is my hope and great prayer that our children will look back one day and say that these evenings of family worship helped to shape their lives, and, even more importantly, were used by the Lord to bring them to Himself.

Appendix A

Sample Family Worship Structures

SAMPLE 1:

Simple Single Day Example

THE WORD OF GOD
Read John 15.

SINGING
Allow the children to pick their favorite hymn.

MEMORIZATION

"Come now, let us reason together, says the Lord: though your sins are like scarlet, they shall be as white as snow; though they are red like crimson, they shall become like wool."

(Isa. 1:18)

PRAYER
Each member of the family pray for the person on their left.

SAMPLE 2:

Family worship for one week

THE WORD OF GOD
Read a chapter per day.

Monday:	Psalm 1
Tuesday:	Psalm 2
Wednesday:	Psalm 3
Thursday:	Psalm 4
Friday:	Psalm 5
Saturday:	Psalm 6
Sunday:	Catch-up Day

SINGING
Sing the same song each day.

HYMN:

"How Sweet the Name of Jesus Sounds"
(Hymn #647 in the *Trinity Hymnal*)

MEMORIZATION
Work on memorizing one catechism question and one selection from Scripture.

CATECHISM MEMORIZATION:

Westminster Shorter Catechism

QUESTION 14:   What is sin?

Answer: Sin is any want of conformity unto, or
             transgression of, the law of God.

SCRIPTURE MEMORIZATION:

"... for the LORD knows the way of the righteous, but the way
of the wicked will perish." (Ps. 1:6)

PRAYER

- Pray for each item on the list every day.

PRAYER FOR THE WORLD

- Pray for the unemployed in our city.

PRAYER FOR THE CHURCH

- Pray for the pastors of our church.
- Pray for missionaries laboring in Morocco.

PRAYER FOR OUR NEIGHBORS AND FRIENDS

- Pray that the neighborhood children would come to saving faith.
- Pray that the Lord would heal Mr. Bruce from cancer.

PRAYER FOR THE FAMILY

- Pray for each member of the family.

Appendix B

Simple Beginnings with Scripture and Prayer

HELP WITH THE SCRIPTURES

Some basic questions to ask small pre-school children when reading the Scriptures:

1. What person or people did we read about (when in narrative, history, or gospel)?

2. What did the person or people do?

3. Was God/Christ in our passage?

4. What did God/Christ do?

Some basic questions to ask elementary-age children when reading the Scriptures:

1. What was our passage about this evening?

2. Did God speak or do anything in our passage?

3. Why did God/Christ say or do that?

4. Why do you think God put this passage in the Bible?

Some basic questions to ask when reading the Scriptures for older children and adults:

1. What does this passage tell us we should believe about God?

2. What does this passage tell us about ourselves?

3. What does this passage tell us about what God desires from us?

4. How does this passage point us to the person of Christ?

HELP WITH PRAYER

A helpful way to pray (ACTS):

1. Adoration of God;

2. Confession of sin;

3. Thanksgiving for God and His good gifts;

4. Supplication (Requests).

A simple intercessory prayer:

1. Pray for something in the world;

2. Pray for your neighbors;

3. Pray for your church;

4. Pray for your family members.

SUMMARY

OF ISAAC WATTS' *A GUIDE TO PRAYER*

Invocation—Call upon God

1. Mention one or more of the names of God—in this way we indicate and acknowledge the person to whom we pray.

2. Declaration of desire and design to worship Him.

3. A desire for His assistance and acceptance.

Adoration—Honor paid to God

1. Mention His nature as God;

2. Mention His many attributes;

3. Mention His many works;

4. Mention His relation to us.

Confession—Recognizing and stating our nature and transgressions to God

1. Humble confession of the lowliness of our original nature; our distance from God, as we are creatures; our subjection to Him; and our constant dependence on Him.

2. Confession of our sins: original and actual.

3. Confession, arising from our sense of all our aggravated sins, that we deserve punishment and are unworthy of mercy.

4. Confession or humble representation of our wants and sorrow of every kind.

Petition and Intercession—Desire of deliverance from evil and a request of good things to be bestowed

1. Pray for the saints;

2. Pray for the church;

3. Pray for our nation;

4. Pray for our friends and relatives;

5. Pray for our enemies.

Pleading—Arguing our case with Him in a fervent yet humble manner

Profession/Self Dedication—Committing ourselves to God

1. Profession of our relationship to God.

2. Profession of our former transactions with God.

3. Profession of our humble and holy resolutions to be the Lord's forever.

Thanksgiving—To give thanks is to acknowledge the bounty of that hand from which we receive our blessings, and to ascribe honor and praise to the power, the wisdom, and the goodness of God upon that account

1. Give thanks for the benefits which God has bestowed on us without our asking.

2. Give thanks for the benefits we have received as an answer to prayer.

Blessing

1. Mentioning the many attributes and glories of God with inward joy, satisfaction, and pleasure.

2. Wishing the glories of God may forever continue, and rejoicing at the assurance of it.

Amen

1. A belief of all that we have said concerning God and ourselves.

2. A wishing and desiring to obtain all that we have prayed for.

3. A confirmation of all our professions, promises, and engagements to God.

4. The hope and sure expectation of the acceptance of our persons, and audience of our prayers.

Appendix C

Resources

PRAYER

A Guide to Prayer (Isaac Watts, Banner of Truth, 2001)

A Method for Prayer (Matthew Henry, Christian Heritage, 1994)

A Praying Life: Connecting with God in a Distracting World (Paul Miller, Nav Press, 2009)

Prayer: A Biblical Perspective (Eric Alexander, Banner of Truth, 2012)

Valley of Vision: A Collection of Puritan Prayers (Arthur G. Bennett, ed., Banner of Truth, 1975)

SONG

HYMNALS

Praise! (Evangelical Press, United Kingdom)

The Worshiping Church (Hope Publishing, 1991)

Trinity Hymnal: Red Cover Edition (Great Commission Publications, 1990)

PSALTERS

The Book of Psalms for Singing (Crown & Covenant Publications, 1998)

The Book of Psalms for Worship (2009)

Trinity Psalter (Crown & Covenant Publications, 1994)

HYMNAL/PSALTERS

The Psalter Hymnal Edition (The Christian Reformed Church, 1987)

DEVOTIONAL/ADDITIONAL HELPFUL BOOKS

365 Great Bible Stories: The Good News of Jesus Christ from Genesis to Revelation (Carine MacKenzie, Christian Focus, 2011)

The Big Book of Questions and Answers: A Family Devotional Guide to the Christian Faith (Sinclair Ferguson, Christian Focus, 1997)

The Big Book of Questions and Answers About Jesus: A Family Guide to Jesus' Life and Ministry (Sinclair Ferguson, Christian Focus, 2000)

Big Truths for Little Kids: Teaching Your Children to Live for God (Susan Hunt, Crossway Books, 1999)

Dangerous Journey: The Story of Pilgrim's Progress (John Bunyan, Eerdmans Publishing, 1985)

The Family Worship Book: A Resource for Family Devotions (Terry Johnson, Christian Focus, 2003)

Long Story Short: Ten-Minute Devotions to Draw Your Family to God (Marty Machowski, New Growth Press, 2010)

The Plan: How God got the World Ready for Jesus (Sinclair Ferguson, Christian Focus, 2009)

WORLD WIDE WEB

Psalms online with music:	http://www.cgmusic.org
Hymnals online with music:	http://www.nethymnal.org
Hymnal online with music:	http://www.hymnary.org

RESPONSIVE READING EXAMPLES

Psalm 1 (ESV)

Blessed is the man
   who walks not in the counsel of the wicked,
nor stands in the way of sinners,
   nor sits in the seat of scoffers;
but his delight is in the law of the LORD,
   and on his law he meditates day and night.
He is like a tree
   planted by streams of water
that yields its fruit in its season,
   and its leaf does not wither.
In all that he does, he prospers.
The wicked are not so,
   but are like chaff that the wind drives away.
Therefore the wicked will not stand in the judgment,
   nor sinners in the congregation of the righteous;
for the LORD knows the way of the righteous,
   but the way of the wicked will perish.

Psalm 61 (ESV)

Hear my cry, O God,
   listen to my prayer;
from the end of the earth I call to you
   when my heart is faint.
Lead me to the rock
   that is higher than I,
for you have been my refuge,
   a strong tower against the enemy.
Let me dwell in your tent forever!
   Let me take refuge under the shelter of your wings! Selah
For you, O God, have heard my vows;
   you have given me the heritage of those who fear your name.

Prolong the life of the king;

    may his years endure to all generations!

May he be enthroned forever before God;

    appoint steadfast love and faithfulness to watch over him!

So will I ever sing praises to your name,

    as I perform my vows day after day.

Psalm 98 (ESV)

Oh sing to the LORD a new song,

    for he has done marvelous things!

His right hand and his holy arm

    have worked salvation for him.

The LORD has made known his salvation;

    he has revealed his righteousness in the sight of the nations.

He has remembered his steadfast love and faithfulness

    to the house of Israel.

All the ends of the earth have seen

    the salvation of our God.

Make a joyful noise to the LORD, all the earth;

    break forth into joyous song and sing praises!

Sing praises to the LORD with the lyre,

    with the lyre and the sound of melody!

With trumpets and the sound of the horn

    make a joyful noise before the King, the LORD!

Let the sea roar, and all that fills it;

    the world and those who dwell in it!

Let the rivers clap their hands;

    let the hills sing for joy together

before the LORD, for he comes

    to judge the earth.

He will judge the world with righteousness,

    and the peoples with equity.

Appendix D

Catechisms and Creeds

CATECHISMS:

Catechism for Young Children

Westminster Shorter Catechism

Westminster Larger Catechism

Heidelberg Catechism

New City Catechism

CREEDS:

Apostles' Creed

I believe in God the Father Almighty,
Maker of Heaven and Earth,

And in Jesus Christ, His only Son, Our Lord,
Who was conceived by the Holy Ghost,
Born of the Virgin Mary,
Suffered under Pontius Pilate
Was crucified, dead, and buried; he descended into Hell
The third day He rose from the dead,
He ascended into Heaven
And is seated at the right hand of God the Father Almighty.
From thence He shall come to judge the quick and the dead

I believe in the Holy Ghost,
The holy catholic Church,

The communion of saints,
The forgiveness of sins,
The resurrection of the body,
And life everlasting. Amen.

Nicene Creed

I believe in one God, the Father Almighty,
maker of heaven and earth, and of all things visible and invisible;

And in one Lord Jesus Christ, the only begotten Son of God,
begotten of his Father before all worlds,
God of God, Light of Light, very God of very God,
begotten, not made,
being of one substance with the Father;
by whom all things were made;
who for us men and for our salvation came down from heaven,
and was incarnate by the Holy Ghost of the Virgin Mary,
    and was made man;
and was crucified also for us under Pontius Pilate;
He suffered and was buried;
and the third day he rose again according to the Scriptures,
and ascended into heaven,
and sitteth on the right hand of the Father;
and he shall come again, with glory,
    to judge both the quick and the dead;
whose kingdom shall have no end.

And I believe in the Holy Ghost the Lord, and Giver of Life,
who proceedeth from the Father and the Son;
who with the Father and the Son together
    is worshipped and glorified;
who spoke by the Prophets.
And I believe in one holy catholic and apostolic Church;
I acknowledge one baptism for the remission of sins;
and I look for the resurrection of the dead,
    and the life of the world to come. Amen.

The Family Worship Book
A Resource Book for Family Devotions

TERRY L. JOHNSON

ISBN 978-1-85792-401-5

Do you struggle to provide enjoyable, meaningful and spiritual times of family devotions? Do you avoid the whole subject but have the nagging thought that you should be doing something?

Let Terry & *Family Worship* equip you for leading your family in worship with the help of some key questions: What is family worship? What have other people done? Why Should I do it? How can I start? A Valuable resource which you will not exhaust in years.

Terry Johnson provides a brief but compelling argument for the importance of family worship, but then takes those he has convinced in theory to the next step: actually putting it into practice! In a day and age when family worship is a rarity, and in which parents who are called to lead in it are not likely to have had personal experience of it in their own upbringing, Johnson's book will prove to be an invaluable aid. May the Lord use this book to bring about a revival of family worship in our land.

Ligon Duncan
Senior Minister, First Presbyterian Church, Jackson, Mississippi

Terry Johnson is Senior Pastor of the Independent Presbyterian Church in Savannah, Georgia.

Christian Focus Publications

Our mission statement –

STAYING FAITHFUL

In dependence upon God we seek to impact the world through literature faithful to His infallible Word, the Bible. Our aim is to ensure that the Lord Jesus Christ is presented as the only hope to obtain forgiveness of sin, live a useful life and look forward to heaven with Him.

Our Books are published in four imprints:

CHRISTIAN
FOCUS

Popular works including biographies, commentaries, basic doctrine and Christian living.

CHRISTIAN
HERITAGE

Books representing some of the best material from the rich heritage of the church.

MENTOR

Books written at a level suitable for Bible College and seminary students, pastors, and other serious readers. The imprint includes commentaries, doctrinal studies, examination of current issues and church history.

CF4•K

Children's books for quality Bible teaching and for all age groups: Sunday school curriculum, puzzle and activity books; personal and family devotional titles, biographies and inspirational stories – because you are never too young to know Jesus!

Christian Focus Publications Ltd,
Geanies House, Fearn, Ross-shire,
IV20 1TW, Scotland, United Kingdom.
www.christianfocus.com